Maxwell Stories

Sam Jaffa is the BBC's Maxwell expert. His investigations into the pension fund's missing millions led him to the secret bank vaults of Switzerland. In Liechtenstein he questioned the man who runs the mystical Maxwell Foundation in the first press conference ever given by a lawyer in that country. In a world exclusive story he uncovered £10 million in shares sitting in an unknown bank account.

Sam Jaffa joined the BBC in 1980 after working on newspapers in Essex. He has worked for local radio in Hull and Stoke and for BBC television in Birmingham. He was a national radio reporter for seven years covering major disaster stories for BBC Radio and Television including the Zeebrugge ferry disaster, the Piper Alpha oil platform and the fire at Bradford City Football Club. He joined the BBC's Business Unit two years ago after working for the corporation in New York. Since then he has covered the majority of the country's financial disasters, the Guinness Affair, Blue Arrow and the collapse of the Bank of Credit and Commerce International.

He lives in London with his wife Celia and their son Lewis.

Ex Libris

Hugh & Georgie O'Shaughnessy

Maxwell
Stories

Sam Jaffa

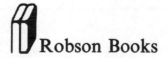

Robson Books

First published in Great Britain in 1992 by
Robson Books Ltd, Bolsover House, 5–6
Clipstone Street, London W1P 7EB

**British Library Cataloguing in Publication
Data**
A catalogue record for this book is available from the British Library

ISBN 0 86051 829 9

Filmset in Times Roman by
Selwood Systems, Midsomer Norton
Printed in Great Britain by
Butler & Tanner Ltd, Frome and London

To Leslie and Dorothy

Acknowledgements

I would like to thank the following people for their help in producing this book.

Louise Botting for the idea. My wife, Celia, for her help and support and my mother-in-law, Eve, for looking after Lewis. Mish Steinberg and Robin Ellison for their advice.

John Pilger, for kindly allowing me to use extracts from his book *Heroes*, published by Jonathan Cape. Roy Greenslade for extracts from his book *Maxwell's Fall*, copyright © 1992 published by Simon and Schuster Ltd and Joe Haines for extracts from his book *Maxwell* published by Little Brown and Co UK Ltd.

Of course, I would also like to extend my thanks to everyone who allowed me to write up their Maxwell experiences. Without their co-operation this book would not have been possible.

Introduction

Everyone has a Maxwell story and it was with this concept
in mind that this book was born. As Joe Haines, a former
Prime Ministerial Press Secretary, said in his biography of
Robert Maxwell: 'If a man is measured by the anecdotes he
generates then Robert Maxwell is very big indeed'.

No one would dispute that. But do these stories tell us
what sort of man he was? I believe they do. If this book has
an aim it is to bring to the reader's attention the different
and often conflicting character traits of this complicated
man. The vast majority of the stories were told to me first-
hand by those who witnessed Maxwell's behaviour. They
show a man who could be cruel one moment and kind and
generous the next; a man of vast wealth, who became a
socialist parliamentarian; a politician obsessed by power, but
who, 20 years after losing his seat, is still regarded by some
as a model constituency MP; a family man who was totally
egocentric; a witty man who, in the words of one of the
union negotiators who fought him over the years, could
'charm the birds off the trees – and then shoot them'.

In trying to fit together the jigsaw pieces of this man's
character I have attempted to obtain first-hand anecdotes
from every sphere of life in which Maxwell operated: from
his early years in Czechoslovakia and the British army,
through his political career, to his rise and fall in the business
world. The stories about him cover the globe from Australia

to America, through Europe and into what was once the Soviet Union.

Maxwell was often tritely described as, 'a larger than life character' – but what a life his was! He was born in 1923 and named Abraham Lajbi Hoch, the third child and first son of a poor Jewish couple living in Ruthenia in eastern Czechoslovakia. Almost immediately the young 'Maxwell to be' underwent his first transformation as the Czech authorities renamed him Jan Ludvick Hoch. As he grew up the young peasant boy had no greater ambition than to own a cow and a field to put it in. He appears to have had no inkling that in April 1991 he was to be named as Britain's seventh richest person, with a fortune estimated at more than half a billion pounds.

At the age of 16 he escaped the Nazis and travelled through war-torn Europe to join the British army. He changed his name and married. Jan Ludvik Hoch, now Robert Maxwell, told his French wife that he would win the Military Cross for bravery, make a fortune and become Prime Minister. He did win the Military Cross, he did make a fortune, and when he became the youngest Labour MP in the 1964 parliament he must have had high hopes of achieving the third of his ambitions.

After the war and during his stint in the House of Commons, Robert Maxwell the increasingly wealthy businessman began to emerge. But in the 1970s Pergamon, the company he had built from nothing, was taken from him and his reputation blighted by a Government inquiry which branded him as unfit to run a public company. He lost his seat in Parliament and his fortune, so that in middle age he had to start all over again. He did so, and the man popularly dubbed 'the bouncing Czech' bounced back with another fortune, bigger than the one he lost.

Maxwell's oft-stated ambition was for his main public company, Maxwell Communication Corporation, to become one of the global communications giants of the 1990s. But his restless drive to achieve this probably led to his downfall.

He borrowed heavily to finance his acquisitions in the United States and then, as recession took hold, he was unable to make his debt repayments. It is only speculation to suggest that Maxwell raided his company's pension funds in desperation. What is known is that on 5 November 1991 Robert Maxwell died while cruising off the Canary Islands aboard his luxury yacht the *Lady Ghislaine*. Some experts believe he fell into the water after having a heart attack and died struggling to get back on board. But other suggestions have been put forward, ranging from the plausible to the outlandish. Some pundits say Maxwell committed suicide because he couldn't face the shame that would follow the inevitable collapse of his business empire. Others have said he was killed by agents of a foreign government. I'm sure he would have enjoyed the mystery.

The uncertainty surrounding Maxwell's death is mirrored in his life. He wasn't the sort of person you could be neutral about – you either loved him or hated him. In this book I have tried to give both views. I have not set out to select anecdotes that vilify him, nor have I wanted to offer a view through rose-coloured spectacles.

Many of the stories are amusing, others contain sinister predictions of Maxwell's future misdemeanours. All, I think, throw large or small shafts of light on the character of this strange man.

Sam Jaffa

Early Years

The man who was to become Robert Maxwell was born in the village of Solotvino, in eastern Czechoslovakia, on 10 June 1923. He was the first son of Mehel and Chanca Hoch, and the third of nine children. His parents were orthodox Jews and young Ludvik, or Laiby as he was known in the family, was brought up in the traditional way.

His father Mehel was an itinerant labourer and was known locally as Mehel der Lange, or Mehel the tall – he was 6ft 5in tall. When Mehel could find work he bought cattle for the local butchers and received the skins in payment. These he sold on to the leather merchants.

It was Ludvik's mother who was to have the greater influence over him. Chanca had taught him to read and write by the time he was four and a half. She hoped he would become a great rabbi, and shortly before his thirteenth birthday Ludvik was sent to a Jewish academy, or *yeshiva*. A year later he moved to a larger *yeshiva* in Bratislava, 380 miles from his home. The year was 1936 and young Ludvik later remembered that he wore patched clothing and had no money. But from then on, his life story reads like a Hollywood film script.

Soon afterwards, the *yeshiva* boy set aside his studies and began selling cheap jewellery. He discarded his traditional long silk coat and his sidelocks. On Maxwell's 60th birthday, Sylvia, one of his two sisters to survive the war, wrote a tribute to him and remembered the *yeshiva* boy growing up.

'I have some early recollections of you when you returned home for visits from the *yeshiva* in Bratislava. I remember your arrival home, probably only a few months after your first departure. We were still living in grandfather's house. I suppose you were about 13 or 14 years old. The incident stuck in my memory because you came with your overcoat pockets stuffed with bead jewellery and trinkets which were, I think, your stock as a part-time travelling salesman. You were selling these things to make a little cash – perhaps the money which paid your fare home. Anyway, I remember this very clearly because you allowed me to choose one of the necklaces from your collection as a present for myself. In our impoverished family presents were unknown; the best I had experienced before then was a new dress or a pair of new shoes for important religious festivals. Your generosity made an impression on me which has lasted nearly half a century.

'The second incident I can remember is your arrival home on a subsequent visit from Bratislava some years later. We had by then moved into our own house in Nagyhely Utca (a quarter of Solotvino largely populated by Hungarians and Romanians). Brana [another of Maxwell's sisters to survive the war] and I went to meet you at the station. When you got off the train we could barely recognize you; instead of the shy *yeshivabucher* we expected, we saw in front of us a flashy young chap, the pre-war central European equivalent of a teddy boy ... no *paiyes* [sidelocks] but a stylish head of hair with all traces of the orthodox young scholar gone. We were amazed and worried about the effect your changed appearance would have on mother. All hopes of her favourite son becoming a rabbi would be shattered. We both advised you to call at a barber's on the way home to have your head shaved. ... You asked us to calm down and to leave to you the problem of meeting mother and explaining your changed personality. You were quite confident she would understand. I am afraid I do not remember the reunion between you and mother, but I assume you were forgiven because she continued to adore you.'

The village of Solotvino was in an area of Czechoslovakia known as Ruthenia. It was an historically troubled part of eastern Europe which, though at the time Czech, had at various eras straddled the borders of Hungary, Poland and Romania. Today it is in the extreme western part of Ukraine.

As war approached young Hoch made plans. It's said he joined the Hungarian underground, but was captured. He was just about to stand trial early in 1940 when he attacked his guard and escaped into what was then Yugoslavia. There he went to the French embassy and volunteered to join the Foreign Legion. He fought for France, but was eventually evacuated to Britain, where he joined the Auxiliary Pioneer Corps – the only unit in the British Army open to foreigners at that time. He began his army career as number 12079140, Hoch, Private L.

Hoch loathed the Pioneer Corps. They seemed to spend all their time digging roads and the young Czech wanted to put down his shovel and pick up a rifle. Luckily, he was befriended by the widow of a colonel in the Ghurka Rifles, who in turn introduced him to Brigadier Gary Carthew-Yorstoun. The brigadier helped Hoch to transfer from the Pioneer Corps to the regular army. Now calling himself Ivan, or Leslie, du Maurier (after his favourite brand of cigarettes), he joined the 6th Battalion of the North Staffordshire regiment. From then on his military career was to move at quite a pace.

Late in 1943 Private du Maurier arrived at Cliftonville on the Kent coast to join his battalion. He was soon promoted to Lance Corporal and was put in charge of a sniper section of about 15 men. The recollections of his army pals give us a picture of du Maurier as a handsome young man with a moustache. He was well liked by his fellow privates and by senior officers but not by sergeant-majors or junior officers. He was regarded as clever and headstrong, a good soldier but one for whom discipline did not mean a great deal. He was viewed as a man who 'could be cheeky but who invariably got away with it'.

Early in 1944 du Maurier was recommended for a commission, but he failed to pass the exam. Three weeks after D-Day the 6th North Staffords sailed for Normandy. In July and August they were involved in a number of battles during which du Maurier was recommended for a commission in the field. He took part in the heavy fighting to secure a bridge over the River Orne and refused to withdraw even though advised to do so by senior officers. The battalion suffered heavy casualties and on 20 August they were moved back from the front line and disbanded.

Du Maurier had been promoted to staff sergeant during the battle on the Orne. He was withdrawn from the line and given another identity as Private Leslie Jones – indeed for a time he had a third identity, that of Private Smith, while operating behind enemy lines. He had a spell as an interpreter at a prisoner of war camp and then went on leave to Paris. It was there that he met Elizabeth Meynard, the woman he married on 14 March 1945.

Elizabeth Meynard became Mrs du Maurier. But in December of that year, when her husband returned to England to be kitted out as an officer in the Queen's Royal Regiment (West Surrey), he did so as 2nd Lieutenant Ian Robert Maxwell. The name Maxwell was suggested to him by his friend and mentor Brigadier Carthew-Yorstoun, who was a proud Scot and thought Maxwell was a sound Scots name.

The Queen's were part of the 7th Armoured Division, the renowned Desert Rats. They were positioned west of the Roer river near Roermond, a Dutch town just inside the border with Germany. On 29 January 1945 A Company and Lieutenant Maxwell moved in to clear the Dutch village of Paarlo. It was here that Maxwell won the Military Cross for his bravery in leading a counter-attack which released a platoon pinned down by the Germans. On 5 March he received his medal from Field Marshal Montgomery.

After a spell of leave he was back in action, and in April he was involved in an attack on the village of Riede on the road to Bremen. The regimental history says: 'A Company led off successfully and by noon had cleared Sudweyne, held by a newly-arrived company of 20 SS Training Division, 7 Platoon (Lieutenant R. Maxwell) alone having killed fifteen SS men and taken fourteen prisoner.'

Maxwell later took part in the assault on Hamburg, Germany's chief port, which was captured on 2 May. That night Germany's surrender was announced. Maxwell's army career continued and in November 1945 he began a new job as an Intelligence interrogation officer at Iserlohn. It was here that his only relatives to survive the war – his two sisters, Brana and Sylvia – were reunited with him.

The work at Iserlohn was so secret that Maxwell took on yet another name to hide his true identity, that of Captain Stone. Early in 1946 Maxwell was recommended for promotion to Captain and in March he was appointed to the Berlin Information Control Unit. In July he was offered an appointment with the Control Commission for Germany as 'a Temporary Officer Grade 3, Information Services Control Branch'. This effectively made him censor of the newly emergent Berlin press.

It was at this point that he began to arrange for his release from the army; and as the door to his army life began to swing shut, so the contacts he had made in Berlin began to open the door to his career as a businessman.

*　　*　　*

Rabbi Hugo Gryn came from the same part of the world as Robert Maxwell. The two met only once – in a lift at London's Central Methodist Hall. It was a small lift and Maxwell wasn't too pleased when Rabbi Gryn got into it. The publisher didn't realize he was in the company of a reverend gentleman and made a less than complimentary remark. Still, the rabbi did have one reason to be thankful to Robert Maxwell.

'Some years ago my daughter was making a television film about my life in that part of what used to be Czechoslovakia from which I originally came. We returned to my place of birth where we were treated like visiting royalty by the local officials. The food in the area was generally awful but they laid on special meals for our camera crew and got rid of any red tape when it came to visits we wanted to make to particular areas.

'We couldn't understand why we were getting such special treatment, until one day we suddenly realized what had happened. The locals had convinced themselves we were making a film about their most famous old boy, Robert Maxwell. He seemed to be venerated almost like royalty.

'I know that once we realized why we were getting such special treatment we should have told them that we had nothing to do with Robert Maxwell. But the treatment we were receiving was so good, and we knew that without it our film would not be made; so I am afraid we left them with the impression that our film was indeed about Robert Maxwell.'

*   *   *

Robert Maxwell was a brave soldier. That is a fact – enough people witnessed his actions and can testify to them. But just how did the man then known as Jan Ludvik Hoch manage to flee his native Czechoslovakia and win the Military Cross fighting for the British Army?

There have been various (and varying) accounts of how the young Hoch evaded the Nazis and travelled west across Europe to join the Allies. In later life Maxwell himself would tell conflicting stories about those years. Indeed, he appears to have made up so many tales about his journey to England that perhaps in the end even he didn't know the truth.

In one version he said he was befriended by and joined members of a Czech underground movement while studying at the *yeshiva* in Bratislava. In another tale he told his army pals that he and his sister had escaped from their home in Czechoslovakia by fleeing to the woods – literally running out of the back door as the Gestapo came in through the front. The rest of the story told of them escaping by 'a devious' route and eventually taking a boat to Gibraltar and then one on to Liverpool!

Maxwell said he acted as a courier for the Czechoslovak underground but was eventually arrested. He was accused of spying and sentenced to death. He was saved by the intervention of the French ambassador – then acting for Czech interests – who successfully pleaded for his life because he was under 18 years of age. On his way to court young Ludvik escaped from his guard by overpowering him (the guard was a World War One veteran with only one arm). While in hiding he met and was befriended by a gypsy, who managed to get our hero's handcuffs off. Ludvik then caught a train to Belgrade. Once in Yugoslavia he joined up with other Czech exiles at the French Embassy and eventually fought in the Foreign Legion before being evacuated to England from Marseille at the fall of France.

Maxwell told this story many times in later life but always with some variations. During his 1987 appearance on Desert Island Discs, the one-armed guard was put in, but the befriending gypsy was out. In the early 1960s one Maxwell press release had him fighting on both the German and Russian fronts at the same time. In another account he explained to his cousin Alex Pearl why he had deserted him just before hostilities began. The two didn't meet again until the war was over, Maxwell told Pearl that he'd met a group of Czech soldiers in Budapest who'd said they wanted to get to France. He agreed to help them as long as they would allow him to go along. They agreed but said he had to maintain total secrecy, so could not go back and tell his cousin where he was going.

Whatever the truth, when young Hoch arrived in Britain in 1940 he joined the Pioneer Corps. Almost immediately he was sent to the Palace Convalescent Home at Ely in

Cambridgeshire to recover from appendicitis. Benita Moxon, then a nurse at the home, describes an 'extraordinary young foreigner' who 'enchanted, fascinated, infuriated and, above all, baffled the lot of us': 'One of the most baffling things about him was the way he seemed to be able to move around as, when and how he pleased. Even the higher ranks in the army were subjected to stringent restrictions in wartime and leave was very limited.

'Ludvik, supposedly a humble private, seemed exempt from all this. He came and went, appeared and disappeared. ... There were many things about him that were inexplicable and nothing seemed impossible. One thing was for sure, he literally and absolutely did not give a damn what anyone thought of him, and that made him enemies.

'Another remarkable trait was that he would attempt absolutely anything, regardless of previous knowledge or experience, or lack of it! One day the resident corporal could not be found to meet a new nurse arriving at the station. Ludvik volunteered for the job and I went with him as a welcoming committee. It was a hair-raising experience. He was 17 and I don't believe he had ever driven a car in his life. After a bit of jiggling around of the gears, we suddenly shot out of the garage backwards, across the main road. We then proceeded to the station in a series of swoops and jolts and life was preserved due to the fact that the little traffic there was, after alarmed glances, gave us a very wide berth indeed.'

Leslie du Maurier, to give him his first army name, is still fondly remembered by many of his comrades in arms. He was a 'tall handsome lad, who was a favourite with the ladies'. He was well liked despite having a reputation as a 'clever chap who was always doing deals'. During the Normandy campaign du Maurier was warned by his superior officers that the Germans were treating captured soldiers from occupied countries as traitors and were sending them to concentration camps when they were captured. In view of this he was instructed to withdraw from the action. Du

Maurier asked for permission to ignore that request – and the permission was later granted. One of his army friends from those days is Harry Shorthose of Darley Abbey, near Derby, who was Regimental Quartermaster Sergeant at the time.

'I remember du Maurier riding around on a German motorcycle he had captured. He went everywhere on it. We were amazed not only that he had captured it but that he never seemed to have any problem finding petrol. Remember, petrol was very difficult to obtain at that time. The bike was destroyed one day when we were bombed by our own side. It seems that du Maurier was riding it when our positions were shelled by our allies the Americans, we think. The bike was destroyed. On the sides of the bike Du Maurier had placed two large baskets which were full of German money, most of it those special promissory notes he'd confiscated; they, too, were destroyed.'

Sam Mitchell recalls an occasion when he and Sgt du Maurier accepted the surrender of 100 prisoners. Du Maurier took all the bank notes the Germans had on them and Mitchell received the small change. At Bayeux, in Normandy, du Maurier was furious when six of his men failed to report one evening at 5pm sharp as he had instructed. The men pleaded that they hadn't known the time because none of them had a watch. The next day he gave each of them a watch, all of them confiscated from German prisoners of war.

After the battle at the River Orne the 6th North Staffords were moved back from the front and dispersed. It was their last engagement. The battalion had lost about half of its men, when the final toll for casualties was made, according to Sergeant Shorthose. He and his friend Sgt Eric Grindley were later sent to Brussels to organize leave accommodation for troops. Some time later one of the soldiers who came on leave was their old comrade, Leslie du Maurier. Shorthose remembers du Maurier borrowing five shillings from his friend Grindley – a debt he never repaid.

'I remember another incident. As the Regimental Quarter-master Sergeant, it was my job to authorize the issue of new kit. I did this by holding inspections known as Clothing Parades – the idea was for soldiers to wear the items of kit they claimed needed replacing so that I could make an assessment. Du Maurier appeared in one claiming he needed a new battledress – that is, the top part of the uniform. I said I didn't think the uniform was that bad and I couldn't authorize a replacement. He didn't argue but simply smiled and walked away. A week later, I saw him again and he was wearing a new battledress – but where he got it from I have no idea. It was typical of him though, he could sell sand to the Arabs.'

His comrades in the 6th North Staffords remember that du Maurier was always losing or damaging parts of his kit. According to Eric Grindley, 'if you gave du Maurier lots of new kit one day, by the next day a third of what you'd given him would have disappeared – Du Maurier sold for cash. He always had his eye on the main chance.'

As we have seen, soon after arriving at Cliftonville, du Maurier was made a Lance Corporal and put in charge of a sniper section. He already exhibited a remarkable talent as a sharpshooter, as Grindley recalls:

'I remember someone bet du Maurier a packet of cigarettes that he couldn't hit a bottle which was floating in water about 150 yards away. He said he could, fired and shattered the neck of the bottle with one shot. The man who bet him said it was a fluke. Leslie du Maurier took aim again, fired and did exactly the same. He hit another bottle in the same place, shattering the neck and winning his packet of cigarettes.'

Many of his army pals tell similar stories of bravado. As the company Quartermaster Sergeant, Grindley had the job of assessing the needs of new recruits like du Maurier. Grindley knew that he was not quite 18 years old when he joined the 6th North Staffords. But after meeting him briefly the Quartermaster Sergeant remarked to his Commanding

Officer, 'We have a guy here who, I'm sure, is going to have your job in the space of six months.'

Grindley remembers the remarkable confidence of the young du Maurier. 'He was as smooth as silk. He could charm the birds off the trees. He was good looking and a hit with the ladies. He was also obviously clever. He spoke perfect English with a slight accent which you couldn't identify. Everyone in the unit looked up to him. If he said jump, they simply asked: "How high?"'

There were two main reasons why du Maurier inspired such confidence. Foremost was because he was supremely confident himself. Part of this stemmed from his language ability – according to Grindley, du Maurier claimed to speak seven languages: Czech, Spanish, Italian, English, French, German and Turkish. He also won over his fellow soldiers because he was a natural leader of men and very brave as well.

'He used to go out with two or three guys at night time and leave them in a safe place behind our lines,' Grindley recalls. 'Then he would go forward himself and get behind the enemy lines. He would invariably pick up a prisoner and bring him back. Du Maurier's German language was perfect. He even went up to a German machine gun post and chatted to them in their own language before taking them prisoner. On one occasion he came back with a Panzer officer and he (Du Maurier) was wearing the German officer's uniform complete with his great coat. He would often go back behind enemy lines wearing that officer's uniform. We became so worried by his behaviour – worried that he would get caught and that his life and the lives of colleagues in the battalion might be in danger if the Germans made him talk – that we issued him with a false identity, in the name of Lance Corporal Smith, with a false number. But it didn't stop him, he still kept going and on another occasion he came back with a German paratrooper's fold-up motor cycle.'

*   *   *

A few years ago, when Robert Maxwell was recalling his war years, he was asked by one of his journalists to explain exactly what they were like. The question came up during a lull in conversation at a lunch. Maxwell then told the story of how he was fighting in northern France when, from behind a hut, stepped a young German soldier armed with a machine gun.

Maxwell said: 'The gun was pointing straight at me. I pointed my gun at him and in German I told him to put it down. He did.'

'What did you do then, Mr Maxwell?' asked one of the guests.

'I shot him dead.'

Maxwell's Business Dealings

As we have seen Maxwell's business career really began back in Czechoslovakia, where he seems to have developed the methods he used for the rest of his life. The war gave him plenty of opportunities to refine these methods, but it was in post-war Berlin that he found his first major opportunities for advancement.

Immediately after the war Maxwell worked as a civilian Intelligence Liaison Officer for the Control Commission, the administrators of the British Zone in Berlin. He became one of 12 British officers chosen to purchase goods, through the American-British Joint Export-Import Agency, to aid the German economic recovery. His role was to buy sugar, coffee, cotton waste (for cleaning locomotives), paint for railway bridges, pigs' bristles for the paint brushes, and railway equipment. Among those who went to Maxwell for help was Julius Springer, cousin of the elderly German publisher Ferdinand Springer. He complained to Maxwell about the inadequacy of Springer's paper ration compared with the allocation for the other newspapers under Maxwell's control. Maxwell threw him out; but some time later Maxwell was introduced to Ferdinand Springer and the two men became friends. Maxwell helped Springer restart his business in Heidelberg and he arranged transport to London for a large quantity of back numbers of Springer's scientific journals. Maxwell set up a company to distribute the journals –

and his career in scientific publishing had begun.

Maxwell left the Control Commission in March 1947 to concentrate on the scientific periodicals distribution business he had set up and on the barter trade he was involved in through a company called Low-Bell, of which he was a director.

In 1948 one of Britain's oldest publishing houses, Butterworth and Company, formed a joint venture with Springer; it was called simply Butterworth-Springer. Maxwell had no financial interest in this company, though he was distributor of its publications. However, it was this company which was to be the foundation of Maxwell's success. During 1951 Butterworths became increasingly unhappy about the partnership with Springer and eventually Maxwell bought the company. He had to change its name, and chose Pergamon, from an ancient Greek city (now Bergama) in Asia Minor.

Maxwell believed, rightly as it turned out, that there would be a great hunger for scientific knowledge after the war. Over the years he steadily built up Pergamon, acquiring a number of companies along the way. In 1959 he moved Pergamon's headquarters to Headington Hill Hall in Oxford, which also became the family home. The building was leased from the council, which prompted Maxwell to boast that it was the grandest council house in England.

Everything appeared to be going well – and then in 1969 came the Leasco affair. Leasco was an American company founded by Saul Steinberg which leased computers to customers. At the time it was said to be the fastest-growing company in the Western world. The company bid for Pergamon but claimed to have been cheated because (they said) Maxwell had inflated Pergamon's profit figures. Maxwell lost control of the firm he had built up. Then, in July 1971, just as he was about to win it back, a Government report into the Leasco takeover dubbed Maxwell 'a person who cannot be relied upon to exercise proper stewardship of a publicly quoted company'. It devastated Maxwell, and for a time it looked as though his business career had come to a premature end.

But city pundits reckoned without his determination and the support from Pergamon's staff. By November 1973 Maxwell had gained a seat on the board, and at the end of January 1974 Steinberg agreed to sell his shares to Maxwell to give him overall control. These shares, valued at 185p only four years before, sold for only 10p. Steinberg had originally paid £9 million for his holding in Pergamon: Maxwell paid him only £600,000 to regain control.

In April 1975 Maxwell became involved in the ill-fated Scottish *Daily News*. The newly launched newspaper was to be printed at the plant of the Scottish *Daily Express* which had closed the year before. Maxwell had agreed to support the *News*, hoping to win points within the Labour Party for backing a workers' co-operative. But the project was flawed from the start and Maxwell, ever the opportunist, got out and moved on.

In 1980 Maxwell quietly began buying shares in Europe's largest printing company, the ailing British Printing Corporation (BPC). By July he had accumulated a stake just below that which Stock Exchange rules would require him to declare. Later that month, in a daring dawn raid, he bought enough stock to increase his shareholding to just under 30 per cent. BPC was losing £1 million a month and everyone thought the company was heading for bankruptcy. The directors refused to allow Maxwell a seat on the board. Lord Kearton, a senior figure in the City, was brought in to act as an honest broker between the parties, but he became convinced that Maxwell, with his firmly expressed ideas about the business and how to handle the unions, was the only saviour possible. In February 1981 Maxwell was voted on to the board as deputy chairman and chief executive. It was at BPC that Maxwell's reputation as a skilful union negotiator was won.

At the end of 1982, BPC was renamed the British Printing and Communications Corporation, emphasizing Maxwell's intention of expanding into cable and satellite television, computers and data banks, electronic printing and every other branch of communications technology. It was now that Maxwell's dream began to take shape: to build a company 'to rank among the world's 10 largest communications corporations'. In September 1987 the name was changed again, to Maxwell Communication Corporation. The idea, Maxwell told the *Financial Times*, was 'not an ego trip. I don't go in for ego trips. It's not my style. It was a decision reluctantly taken. I was forced into it by my colleagues.'

The corporation became Maxwell's main publicly quoted company. His other public vehicle was Mirror Group Newspapers (MGN), which he had acquired from the publishing giant Reed International in 1984 for £113 million. In addition to these publicly quoted companies and their subsidiaries, there were almost 400 privately owned Maxwell companies and probably about a thousand companies in the Maxwell empire as a whole.

Those who had business dealings with him over more than 40 years say that in the early days he was genuinely innovative. He seemed able to perceive and exploit gaps in the publishing market more quickly and more effectively than any of his contemporaries. This gift was also reflected in his shoot-from-the-hip style of management.

Don Fruehling was President of the Maxwell Pergamon Publishing Group in 1988–91 and was responsible for developing Maxwell's publishing interests in the United States. He recalls that his interview for this position – his first encounter with Maxwell – took place on a flight from London to Paris: 'I was in the process of leaving McGraw-Hill, where I was Executive Vice President of the Corporation and President of the McGraw-Hill Book and Broadcast Companies. Through a friend, Mr James Sullivan, who worked for Maxwell in the US, I was dispatched to London to be interviewed by Mr Maxwell to head up his publishing efforts in the US.

'Arriving at his office at 8.30am, I spent the rest of the

day cooling my heels. At 5pm, his assistant informed me
that he was leaving for Paris and would not be able to see
me. After I had expressed my chagrin over this turn of
events, it was decided that I would fly to Paris with Mr
Maxwell and he would interview me during the trip.

'On the flight were two journalists. One was a reporter
from my old company, McGraw-Hill. The *Business Week*
reporter and Mr Maxwell immediately engaged in a terrific
argument over a variety of questions. My interview lasted
10 minutes and I was hired. With a flourish, Robert Maxwell
left me standing at the airport in Paris without a visa to get
out of the country. Not expecting to end up in Paris, I didn't
have a valid visa for either entering or leaving France. After
a confusing and hostile fight at customs I was finally allowed
to leave the country.'

Maxwell could treat those who worked for him very
badly. He would reduce men to tears and would use public
humiliation as a method of instilling fear and docility in his
employees. (One senior executive claimed Maxwell adopted
a three pronged approach: Isolation, Humiliation,
Decapitation.)

Don Fruehling's wife Gudrun saw Maxwell's business
methods at first hand.

'I was with my husband and Robert Maxwell on a business
trip to Moscow. We were travelling in convoy, like the
American President might do, in a number of black limousines. My husband and Maxwell were in one car and I was
in another. We stopped somewhere – I can't remember where
or what for – and Maxwell insisted that I join him and my
husband in their car. He then proceeded to criticize my
husband in front of me – to shout and bawl. I am convinced
the only reason he asked me to join them in the car was so
that I could witness Don's humiliation. Maxwell simply
wanted an audience.'

One day Maxwell was in New York and one of his
American lawyers received a call from one of Maxwell's
assistants asking him to draw up a legal document urgently.

He was given 45 minutes to do it. Unfortunately, Maxwell's office was vague about certain details of the contract, making it impossible to compose a document that would not be far too generalized to be of much use. Some 15 minutes later Maxwell's office rang back to remind the lawyer that Maxwell expected the contract within the half hour. Meanwhile the lawyer was still trying to get more information. With five or 10 minutes to go before the deadline, the phone rang again.

This time it was Maxwell himself.

'Where is that contract?' he demanded.

'I'm working on it, I'll bring it over shortly,' said the lawyer.

'I'm leaving the hotel by helicopter in 15 minutes,' Maxwell responded. 'If you want to keep your job you'd better get that f . . . . . g contract over to me.'

The lawyer knew that Maxwell was staying at the Helmsley Palace Hotel and innocently asked Maxwell which floor he was on. There was a pause, which the lawyer thought was because Maxwell couldn't remember his room number.

Then Maxwell bellowed: 'I'm on a floor high enough that, if you don't get that contract over here as fast as I've told you to, it will hurt when I throw you off.'

Derek Terrington, who is now a media analyst with Kleinwort Benson, fell foul of Robert Maxwell when he was an analyst with UBS Phillips and Drew. Maxwell tried to have him dismissed. In January 1989 Terrington had issued a 'sell' recommendation to investors in Maxwell Communication Corporation, stating that he was unclear how the company's strategy would benefit ordinary shareholders.

'Later that day,' Terrington recalls, 'Maxwell phoned UBS P and D and took away £80 million of pension fund money which the company was investing. Maxwell told my bosses it was because of the unfair criticism of him and his company for which I was responsible. They were pretty upset but quite supportive of me. He also had me banned from any contact with his company and I had to send an assistant any time I wanted to communicate with them.

'When Maxwell decided to float the Mirror Group of Newspapers in early 1991 I was again critical of his plans. I said I thought it was overpriced, that I didn't like the blurring of boundaries between his private and public companies, and that some operations simply didn't make commercial sense, including *The European* and the purchase of the New York *Daily News*. My recommendation was that the shares should not be bought.

'Again he was furious. He decided to ring just about everybody telling them not to have anything to do with me. He harassed me at every turn and even managed to get the main board members of the company (it was Swiss owned) out of their beds in Zurich at four in the morning to complain about me. He also tried to have my credentials revoked by the Securities and Futures' Association. Normally the SFA rubber-stamp those people who are already working as analysts, but Maxwell was trying to prevent me from working again. He bragged to others that this was what he would do. But no one in the establishment took these threats seriously, and I am still working.'

Mind you it may not be so surprising that Maxwell took Derek Terrington's view of the worth of his company's shares so much to heart. The analyst's view was expressed thus: 'Cannot Recommend A Purchase' – think about those capitals!

Paul Ellis ran a company which made corporate films for Maxwell's business empire. He worked for Maxwell for four years, but his most lasting memory of this association is of the first time they met.

'I was ushered into the presence and Mr Maxwell asked me what I knew about the company I was going to produce the film about: the British Printing Corporation.

'I said I didn't know much about it, though I knew a little about him.

'"Do you?" he said. "Well, let me tell you about the man who runs this organization. This man is a great politician. This man is a confidant of world leaders: Brezhnev, Gorbachev,

Gandhi. This man is an artist and a film-maker and this man is the world's greatest businessman. That's what you have to understand if you are going to make a film about BPC.'"

One of the organizations Maxwell bought as he developed his business interests was AGB, a leading market research and survey group that, among other things, measured the audiences for television programmes. These ratings were produced for BARB, a company owned jointly by the BBC and the ITV companies. The Chairman and Chief Executive of AGB was Sir Bernard Audley, who met Robert Maxwell for the first time aboard the *Lady Ghislaine*. AGB had over-extended itself in the United States. To save the situation, Sir Bernard had worked out a rescue deal involving the publishing group MAI, headed by Lord Hollich. Sir Bernard says he was pleased with the deal and was waiting nervously for the Extraordinary General Meeting of the company, which was to take place at the end of August 1988. Share-holders were to be asked to vote on three resolutions which needed to be passed for the deal to go through. The Audley family was due to go to France for their annual holidays, but Sir Bernard was to fly back for the meeting.

A few days before the EGM he received a phone call from a major figure in the City informing him that Robert Maxwell wanted to come and see him.

'The object of our meeting was supposed to be the US mapping project, the TFI sampling situation in France, and a market analysis for *The European* – but none of this really rang true. I knew – as it says in *Lolita* – "where his manic inner eye was fixed". So I put forward the feeble excuse that I was going to France. I was told that he was down in France anyway, at Antibes on his boat.

'"He'll send a helicopter for you."

'I said I was perfectly capable of driving down to Antibes, which I did. I boarded this huge, sleek vessel, the *Lady Ghislaine* and, standing there to greet me, were Robert and Ian Maxwell.

'His opening words to me were: "Sir Bernard, I have 4.9 per cent of your company and I have immediately available to me 10 per cent. I will use these to vote down the resolutions proposed to shareholders at the EGM. I wish to make a cash bid for your company and propose that our advisers get together to discuss terms."

'That was his message to me. It put me right on the spot. At the time my shares were suspended pending the deal. He could wreck the whole thing by frustrating those resolutions at the EGM. He had me over a barrel, so I simply had a discussion with him about terms. I asked him if he intended to break up the company or keep it intact. He said, "I pledge to you that my whole purpose would be to fully resource the company and to keep it intact."

'"In that case," I replied, "I am prepared to discuss a cash bid with you." I promptly upped the terms, which, to his credit, he never sought to waver from, and that is how the company passed into the hands of Maxwell.

'Within a month he started selling off bits of the company.'

Shortly after taking over AGB, I understand that Maxwell called Sir Bernard on the latter's carphone and said he wanted him to stand down as a trustee of the pension fund. Sir Bernard pointed out that he couldn't do that because he wasn't a trustee. He explained that he'd decided that it wasn't right for him to be Chairman and Chief Executive of the company and a trustee of the pension scheme at the same time. Sir Bernard explained that his Finance Director and another senior executive were trustees.

'Right!' said Maxwell. 'I'll be talking to them, because I want Kevin, Ian and myself to replace them as of now.'

Sir Bernard had built up AGB, over 25 years, from a £100 company to a £150 million one. After the Maxwell takeover, Sir Bernard occupied an office next to Maxwell's for two years and was able to observe him at close quarters. He says Maxwell was capable of devoting the minutest attention to detail. He also believes Maxwell realized that a man's office is an extension of his territory and that if you destabilized his territory, you destabilized the man as well.

'When I held my first meeting – I think it was my first AGM under Maxwell – one of the executives prowling the corridors said to me: "Oh, you must be ready for Mr Maxwell. You realize you are going together? He'll want to go to the meeting with you."

'I said: "When Mr Maxwell is ready, he can call for me. After all, we have a connecting door between our offices. No doubt, when he is ready he will let me know."

'"Oh, no!" said the executive. "You must be waiting for him." Needless to say, I wasn't waiting. Actually, for 30 seconds or so I suppose he had to wait for me.

'Next day, the door between our offices had been changed: it had a one-way lock on it.

'You would not believe that a man used to thinking in cosmic terms would have time to accommodate in his mind such trivial things, but that was what he could do.

'In watching Maxwell one observed what I would describe as an atmosphere of total power: the merchant bankers queuing up, sometimes for hours on end, in the lobby of the ninth floor of Maxwell House, waiting to see him; some of the great names of the City waiting interminably, only to be dispatched in minutes. One saw executives waiting on landings to report the progress of the Chairman as he moved from floor to floor. You had here people who were absolutely petrified. The group was run in an atmosphere of total fear. And a lot of people lived their lives in that atmosphere of fear and were perfectly prepared to do so.

'Somebody once asked me how these people could live like that? And I remembered a programme I had seen on the subject of the dung beetle: it is born in excrement, grows up in it, it eats it, it mates in it, gives birth in it and then it dies in it. People lived their lives in that way. Their only concern was not to put their heads above the parapet, to avoid at all costs eyeball contact because if you were noticed you might well go and you might be the last to know about it.

'People might change the carpet outside your office. You would say: "That's a good thing, I didn't know I was going to have a new carpet." Next thing, the wall of your office was being torn down and you would say: "Just a minute, I didn't know we were going to change to open-plan so soon." Then the people doing it would realize you hadn't been told that you were out of the group, you'd got the sack.

'A short while before Maxwell disappeared one of his top executives was summoned to Maxwell House and told he'd lost his job. He got in his car and drove back to his office – only to discover that it had been locked in his absence. This was the behaviour of a man who thinks very big – in fact is overwhelmed by the power of his visions and achievements – but at the same time can think very small.'

Mike Kirkham, formerly head of Television Research at AGB, recalls that shortly after Maxwell took over, 'he called me in and asked me what I was doing about the "Max Factor". I said I was doing nothing. He was worried about what some people saw as a conflict of interests because he owned 20 per cent of Central TV and had now acquired the company which produced the ratings for Central. He told me I must address the issue and he wrote a letter to BARB in which he said that integrity was like virginity – you can only lose it once. I thought that was amusing coming from him.

'I remember one meeting held in the dining room of the penthouse apartment on the top floor of Maxwell House. Kevin Maxwell was in the chair. Before the meeting began I told him I had to get away by three o'clock because I had an important meeting with clients. At about quarter to three Robert Maxwell came into the room and took over the meeting. Fifteen minutes later Kevin leaned across and asked me if it was time for me to go. Robert Maxwell stopped the meeting to ask me why I had to leave. I explained, and he asked who the clients were. I told him.

'He said: "Right, take the helicopter." (There was a helicopter and pilot on 24-hour stand-by.)

'Bob asked me if I knew who owned the land next to the building in which my meeting was taking place, so that he could negotiate landing rights. I said I thought it was owned by Taylor Woodrow Property. He immediately phoned them and asked to be put through to the managing director. I went out of the room and a few minutes later he told me he'd obtained permission to land. When I asked him if I had been right about who owned the land or if there was any uncertainty about it, he said: "If in the future there is any doubt, assume that I own it."'

Such sudden decisions and actions were characteristic of Maxwell. Mike Kirkham again: 'I was once in the middle of a presentation to BARB when a secretary passed me a message from Robert Maxwell. It read simply: "This presentation must cease at once. I want these people out of the building."

'He often used to do things like that. It made life very difficult for you.'

*   *   *

It's said that Maxwell paid up to 30 dollars a share too much for the American publishers Macmillan Inc. One of the reasons was that he had become obsessed with having as large a media empire as the Australian magnate (now a US citizen) Rupert Murdoch. He never did achieve that, but over the years he did many deals with Rupert Murdoch and on numerous occasions he had come out on top.

On one of these occasions Maxwell was in Australia with Michael Richardson of stockbrokers Panmore Gordon (Sir Michael is now Chairman of brokers Smith New Court in London). Maxwell and Richardson had been working and negotiating for three days, getting up at 7am and usually carrying on until 2am the next morning.

The deal was finally signed at midnight. Rupert Murdoch then offered his guests a friendly game of poker. The game began at 1am. On the first hand, Maxwell picked up his five cards and immediately exclaimed, 'Well, I never did! What a hand!' When the dealer asked him how many cards he wanted, Maxwell replied 'These will do.'

The Australians, of course, thought he was bluffing. The opening bid of 100 Australian dollars was quickly raised to a thousand, and then Maxwell raised it to five thousand. One of the Australians decided to call him: 'See you for five thousand!'

Maxwell scooped the pot with a high straight.

Next day Richardson was talking to a pretty fair-haired girl at a party in Sydney. To his surprise, since he had never met her before, she told him that she was very unhappy with him and his business colleague. Richardson asked why.

The girl said: 'Well, I was nicely tucked up in bed with my husband last night when the phone rang. It was Rupert telling him to come over and play poker. "We've got a couple of Poms ready for fleecing." I was upset, but my husband said I could have half his winnings. At breakfast this morning I asked him how much I had won, and he said, "You owe me 30,000 dollars."'

*   *   *

Maxwell was notorious for accepting invitations to functions and not turning up. Indeed, the day before he died I was a guest at the annual Anglo-Israel Association dinner at the Dorchester hotel in London at which he was due to be one of the guest speakers. No one was surprised when he failed to turn up. He usually sent a member of his family to read his speech if he decided to cancel an appearance, and on this occasion his son Ian arrived to perform the chore. It soon became obvious that this particular non-appearance had been planned well in advance. The excuse was that Robert Maxwell had suddenly been struck down with flu, but Ian was too word-perfect with what was supposed to be some-one else's speech for this to be likely. (As we now know, Maxwell had decided a few days before to fly down to the Canary Islands for a short rest aboard his yacht, the *Lady Ghislaine*.)

Another story illustrates this particular failing of Maxwell's rather well. He had been invited to a banker's lunch in the City of London. At about 12.50, some 10 minutes before lunch was due to be served, his host received a telephone call. It was Maxwell, who said, 'I can't make it, I'm in Budapest on important business. I'm sorry but it is impossible for me to get away.'

'That's a shame,' said his host. 'We have the Chairman of National Westminster Bank and the Chairman of Lloyds here and it would have been a great opportunity for you to talk over your business plans with them.'

'I'll be there in 10 minutes,' said Maxwell, and slammed down the receiver.

*   *   *

It has been suggested that Robert Maxwell's death was a bad day for libel lawyers. David Hooper of Biddle & Co disagrees. He defended both Aurum Press and the *Bookseller* against writs from Maxwell and says that, to those who acted against him, Maxwell's use of the libel law raised real problems about the triumph of money and power over the freedom to publish. 'It is often thought that it was only in libel cases that Maxwell lied and cheated. When his sacked employees sued for unfair dismissal, Maxwell was perfectly happy to lie and cheat there as well.'

When he unfairly dismissed Andrew Nopper, a financial director at Caxton Publishing, on half an hour's notice, 'ranting and roaring' when Nopper sought to establish the falsity of Maxwell's charges against him, Nopper successfully sued Maxwell's company for unfair dismissal.

Maxwell knew that ordinarily a claimant could not hope to recover his legal costs in an industrial tribunal. What better than to spin the proceedings out so as to bleed the resources of his former employees? First the case was adjourned to fit in with the great man's diary. Came the day of the hearing, 22 March 1982 – no Maxwell. He was said to be in South Africa, on his way to Japan, engaged on a mission that might save thousands of jobs for the British Printing Corporation workers.

Maxwell got his adjournment. On his way home from court, however, Nopper paid a visit to Maxwell House in Worship Street in the City of London. There was Maxwell's Rolls and his chauffeur; and, yes, the commissionaire confirmed, the great man had spent the day working there.

Nopper knew that one of his fellow directors, Edward Warbey, at Caxtons, who had also been unfairly dismissed, had his Tribunal case coming up in a week's time on 29 March.

'Find out where Maxwell is going to be on the 29th!' Nopper helpfully warned Warbey. On that day the by now customary adjournment was requested and again it was claimed on Maxwell's behalf that he was on a trip to South Africa and Japan.

'Oh, no, he isn't – he's in Oxford at Headington Hill Hall,' Warby was able to say. The Tribunal granted a short adjournment to find out where Maxwell was. When it was established that Warby was right about the great man's whereabouts, Maxwell chucked his hand in. His greatly embarrassed lawyers withdrew from the case and the Tribunal most unusually awarded £1,200 costs against Maxwell for having acted so vexatiously and unreasonably.

One lawyer who worked for Maxwell for three years from 1986, says: 'It wasn't so much his reputation he was concerned with in bringing libel actions, it was that he shouldn't be bested. He wasn't really concerned with what people thought of him, he was concerned to let them know that they couldn't get away with speaking ill of him. Like a lot of company chairmen, he could veer wildly from being interested only at the macro level to being obsessed with trivial details. He was very difficult to work for: either you rowed with him all the time, which was an exhausting experience, or you buckled under. I think he cared for his family, but he was tremendously driven and was indifferent to the feelings and welfare of people around him.

'Unlike many entrepreneurs, there was another side to him. He was deeply interested in AIDS, scientific development, peace in the Middle East and the Holocaust. He once spoke a little Yiddish to me which I didn't understand. He was very good at giving his advisers only a part of the picture.

'He used to drive me mad with his phone calls. He called my house on one occasion and spoke to the nanny. He asked where I was and was told that I was in the synagogue. It was Yom Kippur, the holiest day of the year for Jews. Another time he rang from New York. It was one in the morning. I answered the phone and he said he wanted to talk to me about a libel writ he had issued. It was Jewish New Year and I said I thought he had phoned to wish me a happy New Year. He paused a little and then did just that. I can't believe he didn't know it was Jewish New Year; after all, he was phoning from New York.'

*   *   *

Maxwell became involved in organizing relief to Ethiopia after the nation was stirred by Michael Buerk's television reports that appeared on the BBC in July 1984. Maxwell was determined that he and the *Mirror* would save the starving, and he was helped by Lord King of British Airways, who let him have a plane for his mercy mission at no charge. Lord King himself came to Heathrow at the planned take-off time to wave the publisher off. But at that moment Maxwell was in Oxford watching his football team play Arsenal in the Milk Cup. He arrived at the airport four hours later, posed briefly with Lord King for photographs, then rushed up the steps and flew off to Ethiopia.

When he arrived in the capital, Addis Ababa, he was met by officials who welcomed him on behalf of the government. Maxwell responded with his usual modesty, saying he was speaking for the whole of Great Britain. He spent his first evening at the Addis Hilton watching the video of the second half of Oxford United's Milk Cup clash with Arsenal, which he'd unfortunately had to miss because of his mercy mission to the famine-stricken Ethiopians.

Maxwell was also active in organizing relief to the earthquake victims of Armenia in 1988. One day Lord Vestey, Chairman of the Dewhurst butchers' chain, received a call from Maxwell's aide, Peter Jay, saying he had Robert Maxwell on the line to speak to him. There was a pause while the phone was handed over.

'Then Maxwell said to me: "Look here, I'm flying down to this earthquake and I want to take some bully beef. I thought you'd be just the man to supply it."

'"How much do you want?" I asked.

'"Better make it a ton."

'Well, we sell beef in 12-ounce tins, so I was desperately trying to work out how many tins that would be. It came to about 3,000. After some further discussion I decided that under the circumstances we would donate the beef. Maxwell seemed genuinely moved and kept saying what a splendid chap I was. He then told me to phone his pilot to arrange for the tins to be delivered to the airfield so they could accompany him to the disaster zone.

'I telephoned the pilot and told him of my conversation with Mr Maxwell. The pilot said that the plane was so small that they could hardly get airborne with Maxwell on board and they would never be able to take 3,000 tins of bully beef as well. But he said that if Maxwell had told me to have the beef delivered to the airfield, then that is what I had better do. I said I would arrange that, which I did.

'The mercy mission took off and the next I heard about it was that Maxwell had arrived in Armenia and there were pictures in the papers showing him meeting dignitaries and distributing bandages, foodstuffs, etc. He even praised my efforts once again. A few days later I received a phone call from the airfield asking me if I could arrange to collect the tins of beef that had not been delivered to Armenia.

'"How much is left?" I asked.

'"Nearly 3,000 tins."

'It seems that Maxwell had taken with him only one box of 12 tins. I assumed then that he had also taken only a small amount of bandages and other emergency supplies. The final twist in the story was that we had to hire a plane to take the rest of our meat to Armenia.'

*   *   *

In 1983 Maxwell made a bid for the Leeds-based firm of John Waddington, perhaps best known as the manufacturers of one of the world's favourite board games, Monopoly. The company's Chairman, Victor Watson, refused to see Maxwell. Nor would he let him speak to the rest of Waddington's directors or workforce, fearing that 'if we allowed Maxwell to speak to us he would mesmerize us like a snake and we would all end up agreeing that being taken over by Maxwell was the best thing for us.' He recalls how his workforce had to be convinced that Maxwell's overtures should be rejected. Mr Watson has allowed me to use his own verbatim account of what happened.

'On 17 May 1983 Waddington's was subject to a hostile takeover bid from Norton and Wright, the bingo ticket printers in Leeds. Both companies had to follow prescribed Stock Exchange procedures of formal offer and formal reply, together with the ritual posturings and protestations to the Press and City observers. The first closing date was 17 June. Nobody expected more than a tiny acceptance, as it is normal for the offer to be increased. But I can remember being uneasy on the night of 16 June. We had much more to say to shareholders but we had been advised to hold our fire. "Save your trump cards" was the plan. But I wondered if our adversary might win the tricks, leaving us holding unplayed trumps. I need not have worried.

'At 7.30 on the morning of 17 June I was in my office when my telephone rang. "Robert Maxwell here" intoned that impeccably English accent. He told me that he had decided to bid for Waddington's. "Who are these people, Norton Tampax?" he asked, as he tried to win me over. His theme was that we should not allow upstarts to interfere in the affairs of the major printing and packaging companies. He said he knew that I would prefer to remain independent but that this was no longer an option, and so it would be sensible for me to welcome his bid. He told me that I would be appointed Vice-Chairman of British Printing Corporation and that there would be a seat on the board for my Chief Executive, David Perry. The enlarged company would be stronger and good fortune would be assured for all. I said that we were capable of winning the battle on our own and did not welcome his intervention.

'We arranged a meeting of our managers and the fathers and mothers of the chapels [shop stewards] in our canteen. I explained what had happened and told them what we were doing to defend the company from these wholly unwelcome and opportunistic bids. We had inspired a question from the floor, which came as follows: "If Maxwell wins, what will happen?" I said, "Well, David Perry worked for Mr Maxwell until he couldn't stand it any longer. Let's ask him." David replied: "I will tell you what would happen. He would arrive by Rolls Royce or helicopter. He would gather you all together and tell you that he was now the owner of the company. He would say that the company was basically sound but that there had been bad management and insufficient investment. But he, Robert Maxwell, would invest, would bring in good management, would provide work, and the future of the company would be assured. Then, a few months later, they would arrive from Head Office to declare redundancies."

'From the back of the canteen a man stood up and said, "My name is Eric Gill. As most of you know, I am the local secretary of the SLADE Union. And I have never found myself so much in agreement with a boss before. I will tell you what happened with the firm of T. and T. Gill here in Leeds. Mr Maxwell acquired the company and, just as Mr Perry says, he arrived by Rolls Royce to address the work-force. He told them that the company was basically sound but that there had been bad management and insufficient investment. But he, Robert Maxwell, could put all that right. There would be investment, work from the BPCC companies, and a bright future for T. and T. Gill. Then, a few *days* later, some people arrived from the BPCC Head Office to declare redundancies and a wage reduction for the rest. I telephoned Mr Maxwell to remonstrate with him and said, 'Tell me this is a mistake.' But Maxwell simply said, 'Things are not as I thought they were,' and put the phone down."

'Eric Gill's intervention had an electrifying effect. Mr Maxwell had developed a reputation for getting things done and his earlier misdeeds seem to have been overlooked by many people. Now, our people were given a timely reminder. We were united against a common enemy.'

Towards the end of 1983, as the bid for Waddington's rumbled on, there was a great deal of fuss about the shareholders' register. Maxwell wanted to know exactly who the major shareholders were, so that his campaign to take over the company could be waged more effectively. An up-to-date list of shareholders eventually had to be sent to the bidders and was delivered to a Maxwell subsidiary in Leeds.

Victor Watson remembers with some amusement that after the bid had lapsed the precious document was returned by the Post Office to John Waddington. It had had insufficient postage and Maxwell House had simply refused to accept it!

David Perry, Waddington's Chief Executive, had worked for Maxwell for six months. Maxwell said he wanted to do great things with Perry. On one occasion he suggested that they should buy all the label companies in England. Perry told him that BPCC did not need any more label companies.

Maxwell asked: 'Well, what is the thing to do?'

'Get into plastics.'

Maxwell said: 'All right, David, go out and buy some plastic companies.'

It was at that moment that Perry realized he was dealing with an unguided missile.

* * *

As Bob Cole, formerly Press Officer of Maxwell Communication Corporation, points out: 'Whatever else is said about Robert Maxwell, he tended to treat everyone in the same way. I remember one day he said he had some important mail that had to go out by mid-day Saturday. It was late Friday and after telling me there were two or three hundred envelopes he asked: "Would you like some help?" I said that would be nice if any were available. He said he'd fix it. I went out of the room and when I came back there were my three assistants – Lord Silkin – former Attorney General – a cabinet minister and a peer of the realm – all ready to help me stuff envelopes!'

* * *

A senior Maxwell executive in the United States recalls the occasion when he was due to accompany the publisher on a trip to the West Coast. Maxwell flew in on Concorde, arriving in New York at about 11pm. He told the executive he no longer wanted to go to California and asked him to book hotel accommodation. The executive knew that Maxwell's preferred overnight stop was the Waldorf Astoria and that Maxwell stayed only in the Presidential Suite at $3,500 a day and all the high-tech communications systems that Maxwell insisted on cost a further $40,000.

The executive phoned the hotel and was told that the suite was available. Before they left the airport the executive phoned a man who worked for Maxwell Communication Corporation in Westchester County and who doubled up as Maxwell's valet when the media tycoon was in New York.

When the executive and Maxwell arrived at the hotel, the valet was already there, resplendent in his tuxedo. Maxwell announced that he was thirsty.

'Yes, Mr Maxwell, what can I fix for you?', the valet asked.

'I'd like watermelon.'

The valet pointed out that it was a cold April night in Manhattan and asked where Mr Maxwell thought he might be likely to find watermelons. Maxwell told him to take the car and go down 2nd Avenue and not to come back until he had found some uncut watermelons.

After the valet had left, the executive turned to Maxwell and told him sarcastically that he was surprised that they had both been in the hotel suite for an hour and that the valet had neglected to obtain watermelon in that time! Maxwell took this quite well and both he and the executive had a laugh about Maxwell's high-handed request. But about 20 minutes later the valet returned to the suite carrying two plates, and sitting on each was an uncut watermelon.

Maxwell turned to the executive and simply said: 'See!'

On another occasion, the same executive remembers, Maxwell was holding a dinner party in his suite at the Waldorf and the valet was once again helping out. The executive mentioned that the valet was a well-known homosexual, and later in the dinner Maxwell turned to the valet and said: 'I'm worried about you.'

'Why is that?'

'It's this AIDS thing,' said Maxwell.

'Oh, you don't have to worry about that, Mr Maxwell,' said the valet. 'Working for you, I don't have time for sex.'

*   *   *

Robert Maxwell was proud of his adopted country, and his family believed that nowhere else in the world would he have been able to succeed as he did in Britain. Indeed, Maxwell once shouted at a heckler who'd pointed up his foreignness during a political rally: 'I chose to be British – you are British by accident.'

With his gift for languages he made a pretty good fist of

disguising the fact that he wasn't British by birth. At times he demonstrated an extremely sophisticated use of the language, but on other occasions he would make the sort of error that showed that English was not his native tongue.

Victor Watson remembers a typical example: 'One interesting feature of the bid from Mr Maxwell for our company in 1983 was the effort to persuade shareholders in the final stages. We were able to get a number of them to announce their intentions (whether they would accept or reject Maxwell's offer) before the closing date, and this tactic hadn't been used before. Mr Maxwell said on television that I had thrown him a googly, which gave us a clue that he wasn't an Englishman after all.'

This is a fairly typical Maxwellism – a botched attempt to use slang. Here are a few examples of his gift for misquotation:

'Jerusalem wasn't built in a day.'

'I can charm the trees off the birds.' (This one was interestingly elaborated by Bill Keys, the former General Secretary of the print union SOGAT '82: 'Bob Maxwell can charm the birds off the trees – and then shoot them.')

'He has made his apple pie bed and he must lie in it.'

'You are running around like chickens without necks.'

'One swallow doesn't spring make.'

The comment about charming the trees off the birds was made to Raymond Walker, a former board member of the British Printing Corporation: 'When Maxwell took over BPC and began building the company into what became Maxwell Communication Corporation he invited me to join his main board. He then decided he wanted me to work from his Oxford headquarters at Headington Hill Hall. On my first day there he was away. But on the second day he met me and asked if I had been given an office.

'"Not yet, Chairman."

'He said: "Come with me." He took me to an office on an upper floor, on a corner with a huge desk and quite magnificent views of the city of dreaming spires. There was a young man sitting behind the desk, and Maxwell said to him:

'"Kevin, get yourself another office, Raymond Walker is going to have this one." Kevin didn't say anything; it was almost as if he expected it. It showed me the kind of relationship he had with his son.'

*   *   *

One of Maxwell's close aides once gave this advice to a newcomer to Maxwell's media empire: 'There is only one thing you have to remember when you work for Robert Maxwell. You have to remember that to him there are only two kinds of people: Robert Maxwell and everyone else – and that includes his family.'

*   *   *

Maxwell was not a man to be underestimated when he wanted something. At the time of the negotiations which led to his takeover of the troubled British Printing Corporation, Maxwell was trying to obtain agreement from all interested parties for his rescue package. The Post Office Pension Fund held valuable loan stocks and Maxwell's deal meant asking the Post Office to accept less than their true value for them, because they had to be repaid before the rest of the deal could go ahead. But the Pension Fund managers didn't believe this was in their fund's interests. However, Maxwell went over their heads directly to the chief executive of the Post Office Pension Fund. Maxwell explained to him that the fund managers were in danger of scuppering the whole deal. He illustrated the point by asking if the chief executive would like to know what the papers would make of the story. He threw on to the desk a copy of a newspaper with the headline: 'Post Office Pension Fund costs BPC 18,000 jobs'. Maxwell made it clear that would be the headline in the papers the next day if the pension fund managers didn't change their minds. As you would expect, it was a powerful reminder of the public interest in the survival of BPC and the fund managers eventually altered their views.

There is no doubt that Robert Maxwell was a convincing orator. He used this talent well in both his political and business careers. He seemed to have the particular knack of being able to reel the most complex set of figures off the top of his head.

A business colleague once described Maxwell as 'the sincerest liar I ever met'; another said he was 'the best actor I ever met.'

In the 1970s Gordon Brunton ran the Thompson Organisation – a vast media empire which included publishing companies, the Times group of newspapers and Thompson Holidays.

Some time after Maxwell's fateful written drubbing from the Board of Trade Inspectors Maxwell approached the Thompson Organisation with what Sir Gordon describes simply as 'a deal'.

'I'd known him for a long, long time and was distrustful of Bob. But my Chairman, Roy Thompson, said I was being unfair. He said both he and Bob Maxwell were foreigners and he knew how difficult it must have been for Maxwell to achieve what he had done.

'Roy Thompson was a kind, intelligent man and though a successful businessman he was sometimes taken in by salesmen. I was the company Chief Executive and thought it was my duty to protect him. So after he'd decided to see Maxwell I asked Roy to humour me and to make notes at the meeting. I suggested that every time Maxwell mentioned a figure or a hard fact Roy should write it down. He couldn't understand why but agreed to do what I asked.

'Maxwell arrived and even by his standards it was a magnificent performance. He wanted us to help him win Pergamon back from Saul Steinberg. He rattled off a string of facts about the financial implications of the deal. Maxwell's talk lasted 35 or 40 minutes and at the end of it I could see that Roy Thompson was impressed. He looked across to me.

I asked Bob if I could just confirm with him a few of the details. I asked him questions about sales, cashflow, turnover and that sort of thing. Roy Thompson then thanked Maxwell for coming to see us with his proposals and said we would be in touch.

'When Roy Thompson and I were alone he expressed his surprise at the presentation and confirmed what I already knew – that the set of figures Maxwell had given us at the end of the meeting were totally different from the first set. Maxwell was an incredibly convincing salesman. Facts didn't matter to him – what he was interested in was creating an atmosphere. He used to make up figures which sounded convincing. Fortunately, we didn't get involved with his scheme.

'When Maxwell was negotiating to buy the ailing British Printing Corporation, I remember thinking he was probably the only businessman in the country who could tackle the terrible problems with the unions. During the delicate negotiations an article appeared in the newspapers which seemed to me to do great damage to him. It claimed that should Maxwell manage to buy BPC, none of Thompson's massive printing orders would be placed with them. Now, the Thompson Organisation's print demands were huge; we were massive buyers of print with items like the Thompson Holidays winter brochure. But such was the state of the printing industry in Britain at the time that quite a lot of our orders were going abroad.

'Anyway, I phoned Bob and said that, although we'd had our differences in the past, I would support him in his bid to win control of BPC and ensure that, provided he was competitive on price, he would get a fair share of our business. I told him I would send him a letter which he could show to the unions and to his bankers, National Westminster, if this would be useful. He said it would be of immense help.

'In the end he acquired BPC, and rang me up virtually in tears. He asked: "Why did you do it? What can I do for you?"

'I said: "Nothing, Bob," and I told him that I thought it

was in the country's interests that he buy BPC and that the newspaper article had simply been unfair. I added that if he could give me a little time, I would be as good as my word about printing opportunities for BPC.

'I called in many of our print buyers and told them – subject to price and quality – to back BPC. This resulted in a significant stream of business to Maxwell, including the contract to print the Thompson Winter Holiday brochure.

'About eight or nine months later I started getting calls from the various managing directors of companies within the Thompson Organisation that were now doing business with Bob Maxwell. They said Maxwell had told them that there was to be a significant increase in prices. When they questioned Maxwell about the increases, he told them not to rock the boat because I, as Chief Executive of the group, had instructed everyone to give Maxwell the work in the first place and that this price increase was part of the original deal.

'I rang Bob and said: "Well, Bob you've done it again! You've screwed it. Why can't you leave it alone?"

'You see, everything was going along nicely. He was doing a good job with the printing work for us, and he was making a fair profit. But he wasn't content with that. He saw an opportunity to make more money. He thought he'd use the threat of my influence, my supposed backing, to scare my managers into accepting higher prices so that he could increase his profits. That's how he operated in his own company: he ruled by fear. I told him that in the Thompson Organisation we didn't work that way, and that each of my managers was free to negotiate whatever contract they wanted to. The effect of all this was that he lost most of the contracts he'd gained from us.

'The problem was that Maxwell thought everyone used his sort of tactics; but of course in a civilized society they don't. It was just one example of Maxwell's self-destructive capability.'

*　　*　　*

In Maxwell's early days his opponents expressed doubts that he had held the rank of captain in the army or had been awarded the Military Cross. It prompted him to obtain affidavits from his comrades as to his bravery, and on one occasion he produced a photograph showing him receiving his MC from Field Marshal Montgomery. From that time few doubted his courage. In later years it was even said that he was as courageous in business as he had been on the battlefield.

He often had to travel all over the world to make deals for Pergamon. As he was about to board a plane for a flight from Mexico City to Acapulco a Mexican official – bribed, according to Maxwell, by fellow travellers who wanted to get on an overbooked flight – told him and his companion, Michael Richardson, that they would have to give up their seats.

The argument about who was to get on the plane took place at the edge of the tarmac, and Maxwell simply marched past a circle of protesting officials and up the steps to the plane. At the top a Mexican policeman whipped out his revolver and pointed it at Maxwell's stomach and told him not to move. Maxwell told him he was going to board the plane and the Mexican threatened to shoot him. For half an hour Maxwell stood in front of a cocked and loaded revolver. He was adamant that the plane would not leave without him. Eventually officials removed two other passengers from the plane and Maxwell and Richardson were able to reclaim their seats.

*   *   *

Maxwell thought of himself as an astute player of the Stock Exchange. He always claimed that he had avoided the stock market crash of 1987, though many were sceptical. However, apparent confirmation of his story came from Brian Chapman, a former Director of Mirror Group Pensions Trust Limited, when he gave evidence to the House of Commons Social Security Select Committee inquiry into the

Operation of Pension Funds. In the few years before his death, investments by Maxwell company pension schemes were made through a Maxwell-owned company, Bishopsgate Investment Management. As Mr Chapman recalls, 'Robert Maxwell was recognized as a decision-maker for Bishopsgate Management and pulled off some very startling coups in terms of investment. In September 1987 he told us quite categorically that the market was going to crash and suggested that we switch 25 per cent of our equities into gilts and raise cash, which we did. By 1st October I was getting a little twitchy, but by the 17th and 18th October I realized what a very good decision that was. There were several other occasions subsequently when Mr Maxwell put propositions to the trustee board and to BIM that subsequently improved the performance of the fund, there is no doubt about it.'

* * *

According to Nick Grant, one of Maxwell's close aides, 'Robert Maxwell was always losing papers and documents, or rather they could not be found at the time he wanted them. One day a "paperchase" was going on in the office. Everyone was looking for a document which authorized a particular payment. The sum involved was rather large and Mr Maxwell had made it clear that when he found out who'd made the payment there would be trouble: he viewed the whole deal as a disaster. The searching continued for a long time, but eventually a photocopy of the original authorization turned up. It had Maxwell's signature on it. The document was placed before him. For a few seconds he was speechless. Then he yelled: "Who the hell let me find this now?"'

He could also be very charming. Mike Kirkham was due to go to Spain on business and had arrived at Heathrow Airport when he received a call telling him to go straight to Maxwell House, where the great man was waiting for him: 'When I arrived I was only kept waiting a few minutes, which in itself was remarkable, as people were often kept hanging around for hours before gaining an audience.

'I walked into his office. Robert Maxwell strode across the room, grabbed hold of my arm and said: "My dear boy, good to see you. I simply had to have this meeting and to hold it without you would have been like having Hamlet without the Prince."'

*   *   *

In 1971–2, shortly after the DTI report, Bob Murphy, then Chairman of Beecham Pharmaceutical, was playing golf with a friend and business colleague. Robert Maxwell had been very much in the news and Bob Murphy casually told his playing partner that he had got to know Maxwell shortly after the war when both were in the Army's Control Commission in Berlin. Murphy said he'd known him for three years and for a year they'd shared a room together. Murphy said Maxwell had been into absolutely everything: 'I can't tell you what a rogue he was. Have you ever seen that film, *The Third Man*? Well, he was just like that character, Harry Lime.'

'Surely you don't mean he was selling watered-down penicillin?' his friend asked incredulously.

'No,' responded Murphy, 'But he was into everything else – and you must remember that at that time human life was cheap.'

*   *   *

Maxwell had a talent for negotiating. He used to vary the pace to suit himself: sometimes slow, sometimes very quick so that the other side would be put out. Nick Grant gave me an example of how Maxwell put subtle pressure on his opponents.

'It was about 9 or 10pm during some labour negotiations which had been slowly grinding away all day. Maxwell suddenly said that he thought we had gone as far as we could and that it was about time we had something to eat before resuming. People knew from past experience that when Maxwell ate he provided a great spread of food. Sure enough it appeared on the table. Maxwell began to tuck in. After some time he said: "Aren't you going to send out for something?"'

*   *   *

Many of those who worked for Robert Maxwell can testify to his tremendous work-rate. Every day was a working day to him: he worked 17 hours a day, seven days a week, and he took no notice of public holidays. He expected the same kind of dedication from those who worked for him. As in all aspects of his life, he used technology to help him get what he wanted. He would instruct his secretaries to go to any lengths to track someone down if he wanted to speak to them, and he almost resented other people enjoying their leisure time.

Sir Bernard Audley says he was once tracked down on a golf course in Spain though he refused to go back to England. But then Sir Bernard had what Robert Maxwell described as S.O.B. ('sod off, Bob') money. In other words his deal with Maxwell was such that he didn't have to do what he was told. One US executive said that if Maxwell found himself for some reason without a phone or if he couldn't phone someone he wanted to speak to urgently he would 'go nuts'. There are many examples of Maxwell ringing people in the early hours of the morning, often just to ask them the time. Several US executives claim he particularly liked to phone people there during American holidays like Thanksgiving.

*   *   *

Maxwell delighted in messing people about. Paul Ellis of Crown Communications remembers when he was once a victim.

'I was due to see him at 11 o'clock and I waited until 12.20. Then I said to one of his secretaries that I couldn't wait any longer and that I had to get back to my office. The journey back took about an hour. I was half way there when the car phone rang. It was Maxwell himself.

'He said, "Where the f..k are you?"

'"I'm going back to the office. I couldn't wait for you any longer."

'"Come back here now!" he ordered. So I just turned the car around and drove back. I often wonder why I did it, but Maxwell had that sort of effect on people.'

Because of the problems of getting meetings with Maxwell during the week, many people decided it would be best to try to see him at weekends when he wasn't quite so busy. Paul Ellis did that one Saturday. They agreed to meet at 9.30 in the morning at Headington Hill Hall. Ellis arrived at about 9 o'clock and was shown up to Maxwell's offices. As he approached he could hear Maxwell's voice. The door to the room Maxwell was in was slightly ajar and he could clearly see Maxwell talking to one of his secretaries.

'Then he disappeared, and a few minutes later I heard him approaching from the opposite direction. He saw me and said: "What are you doing here? Those f.....g secretaries, why didn't they tell me you were here?"'

*   *   *

Apparently one day Robert Maxwell was in the middle of a board meeting when the telephone rang. He picked it up and said: 'Yes.' Then, after a pause, 'Half-past three.'

Afterwards he explained what had happened. The telephone caller had asked if that was Laura Ashley and then inquired at what time the store closed.

*   *   *

Keeping people waiting was just one of the ways in which Maxwell exercised power and reinforced his status as a very important person. On one occasion a man had been sitting outside Maxwell's office for about two hours. He was eventually allowed into the divine presence. Charmingly, Maxwell apologized for keeping him waiting and asked if he'd like a coffee.

'No,' replied the visitor, 'I've just had one outside.'

'Splendid,' said Maxwell, 'black or white?'

*　　*　　*

Maxwell regarded himself as a head of state and therefore it was quite acceptable for him to have people hanging about waiting for an audience. In some cases senior executives or City advisers might have to wait all day without gaining an audience. They would then have to do the same thing the next day and even for a third day before being ushered into the presence.

Another of Maxwell's foibles was to make sudden decisions to rush off to places, often carrying those waiting to see him along in his wake. Stephen Parnell was formerly managing director of a Maxwell company called Syndication International, which sold stories that had appeared in the Mirror Group papers to other newspapers around the world. Senior executives in the Maxwell organization used to be allocated a particular day and time each week when they would report progress and problems to Maxwell personally.

Stephen Parnell was waiting for his appointment with Maxwell when he was told, not unusually, that Maxwell was behind schedule. One of Maxwell's assistants told him to come with him if he wanted to see the great man.

'I was marched out to the helicopter and told to get in the back. Maxwell appeared and the helicopter took off. We had our discussion flying up to Headington Hill Hall. When we got there I was simply dropped off in a field and told to find my own way back to London. That sort of behaviour was typical of Maxwell. Indeed, I lost my job while I was on business in South Africa. It was just before Christmas and I received a call saying there was no need to come back – in effect telling me I had been fired. I was told that my contract ended as of that day. There was no explanation, but then when you joined Maxwell's organization that is rather how you thought things would end anyway.'

*　　*　　*

Mike Kirkham and the newly appointed Chief Executive of AGB were on one occasion told by Maxwell to fly to New York on Concorde for an important meeting. During the flight Kirkham asked his boss when the meeting was to be held and where. He was told that Maxwell had said they'd be given details on arrival. All they had to do once they were through customs was phone the number they'd been given.

Because the new Chief Executive was American he was able to get through the airport arrival formalities quicker and was on the phone when Kirkham emerged. The Chief Executive put down the phone, turned to Kirkham and said Maxwell had cancelled the meeting.

*　　*　　*

Maxwell succeeded in fooling many people by publicly announcing a generous gift or a multi-million pound deal. But, as they say: 'You can fool some of the people some of the time, but not all of the people all of the time.' And some people are harder to con.

Yigor Yakovlev, who now heads Russia's state television service, once worked for Maxwell's *Moscow News*. A close friend of Mikhail Gorbachev, Yakovlev remembers the Soviet President complaining to him that so many Western businessmen had promised to help the Soviet Union but few had delivered. Both laughed when Gorbachev called it the 'Maxwell syndrome'.

*　　*　　*

Towards the end of Robert Maxwell's life, many of those who knew him intimately report seeing a marked change in his behaviour. His wife, Dr Elizabeth Maxwell, told close friends that the Maxwell she knew over the last 18 months of his life was not the man she married. Others, too, noticed a change. Some say it began when he took over the New York *Daily News*; some say he started to change six months or a year before that. Surprisingly, many noticed a mellowing of Maxwell's character.

Bob Cole, his loyal Press Officer, worked for Maxwell for a total of 30 years and says he spent more time with the publisher than he did with Mrs Cole! In his years as Press Officer Bob Cole prepared more than one million press releases. He says that 99 per cent of them, no matter what the subject, began: 'Robert Maxwell, Chairman and Chief Executive of ...'.

'My last meeting with him took place on Wednesday, 31 October 1991 – five days before his death. He sent for me at about 7.45pm. He told me he was going away for a short while on the boat and he wanted to see me to make sure (as he put it) "everything was up to date".

'I told him I had no problems. On that particular Wednesday there had been an editorial lunch. He used to love attending these – all the group's papers' senior editorial staff would be there. Mr Maxwell would have a chance to give them his views on particular subjects and listen to their comments and concerns.

'He was describing events to me when he said: "Oh, by the way, I think you might like to know all the editors were very generous in their praise today about the way you handled the Seymour Hersh Israeli arms-dealing story."

'As you may remember, Hersh's book *The Samson Option* suggested that Mr Maxwell had a hand in turning in Mordechai Vanunu, an Israeli technician who sold information and photographs about Israel's "secret" nuclear bomb to the *Sunday Times* in 1986. There were also further allegations that Mr Maxwell was involved in arms deals on behalf of Israel. When the story broke Robert Maxwell was in America so I had to deal with press calls.

'Anyway, after passing on what the editors had said Mr Maxwell added: "They were fulsome in their praise and may I add my thanks. I am very grateful."

'I thought: "My God, that is praise indeed coming from him." But I was waiting for the sting in the tail. Sure enough, as we were walking to the door of his office he said: "But you still haven't learnt, have you?"

'"What, Mr Maxwell?" I asked.

'He said: "You still seem to think that the role of a press officer is to assist the press, but fail to grasp that the role of Robert Maxwell's press officer is to hinder the press."

'He smiled and then added: "But anyway, thank you very much." He then put his arm around my shoulder and walked me to the front door. There he gave me a big hug and said: "Cheerio."

'That was the last I ever saw of him; and, looking back on that meeting now, I can't help feeling that somehow he knew it was going to be our last.'

Publishing

Pergamon Press, the scientific publishing company which Robert Maxwell built from scratch after the Second World War, was the mainstay of Maxwell's business empire. Over nearly 40 years he built it into the world's second largest scientific publisher, and throughout most of that time it produced healthy profits which allowed Maxwell to expand his interests elsewhere.

In 1951, Maxwell borrowed £13,000 to buy the small company he named Pergamon, (In March 1991 it would be sold to the Dutch publishing giant Elsevier for £440 million.) At the time Maxwell bought Pergamon he was keen to establish himself with the British publishing elite. As a step towards achieving this he agreed to take a problem off their hands: a loss-making wholesaler called Simpkin Marshall. But within four years it failed, owing £556,000, and the Official Receiver criticized the directors – including Maxwell – for delaying the closure of the company.

Inside the publishing world Maxwell quickly gained a reputation as an arrogant showman, the exact opposite of the staid image of the typical British publisher of the 1950s. Meanwhile he was developing a powerful company in Pergamon. He had realized that the world was crying out for information on the fast-moving post-war developments in science and technology. What is more, many of Pergamon's journals proved to be highly profitable because academics often competed for the honour of writing in them. They would write for little or no payment (sometimes they even paid Pergamon for the privilege of publication), and the universities and science-based companies could not afford not to pay the high subscription rates if they wished to keep up with the latest advances in their fields of scientific research.

By 1964 Pergamon was publishing 600 book titles a year and 70 journals. It was floated on the Stock Exchange with a value of over £4 million, and all went smoothly for a few years. Then in 1968 Maxwell was rebuffed by shareholders in his bid to buy the *News of the World* – forced to concede victory, not for the last time, to his arch-rival Rupert Murdoch.

The following year Maxwell attempted to merge Pergamon with the American company Leasco, headed by the even younger, even more successful Saul Steinberg. The idea was that Pergamon's scientific database could be loaded into Leasco's computers. But while Leasco's accountants were having difficulty obtaining information from Maxwell, it emerged that two of Maxwell's family trusts had been selling Pergamon shares that had been bought by Leasco at inflated prices. Leasco then discovered that a large proportion of Pergamon's profits derived from dealings with private Maxwell companies, which cast doubt on their true value. Leasco withdrew its £25 million bid, but by then it held 38 per cent of Pergamon's stock. Leasco banded together with institutional investors to vote Maxwell off the board. The damning criticism of Maxwell in the report of the Board of Trade inquiry into the affair haunted him for the rest of his life.

*　　　*　　　*

On the first of April 1973 Robert Maxwell returned triumphantly as Chairman of Pergamon. His first day back was also the first day at Pergamon for Richard Charkin, a 23-year-old graduate at the beginning of his publishing career. The young Charkin was employed as Senior Publishing Manager (Life Sciences). (He is now Chief Executive of the Octopus Publishing Group.)

'I remember we all worked in one huge room like an aircraft hangar. It was very strange to me because I had been used to the Dickensian atmosphere of publishing offices in central London. There was a tannoy system, and on my first day Maxwell's voice boomed out and announced that it was our Chairman speaking. Everyone was herded into the canteen; there must have been about 300 people there. Maxwell told us the previous management had been hopeless, but that now he was back, Pergamon was to become the most successful company of all time. He told us that people who worked hard would succeed – and those who didn't work hard would be sacked.

'Maxwell's room at Pergamon was memorable. Most Chief Executives of a publishing company have one commodity aplenty – books. But on Maxwell's shelves there were only spines – the books had no pages or text. There was also one unusual item of furniture – a chess board. The pieces were set out to represent one of the classic Grand Master games of the past. Maxwell used to make a move every day, but it was obvious he couldn't play at that level – and in any case, who was his opponent? The strange thing was that Maxwell wanted people to believe that he played chess at a much higher level than he did. But why? In any case, if people just walked past the board, very few of them would be able to appreciate the subtle difference between one of the most important recorded games and, say, a friendly game of chess between two third formers.'

Charkin was also impressed with Maxwell's somewhat novel approach to business. 'If a company wrote in asking if Pergamon wanted photocopying machines, he would reply asking them if they required scientific books for their company library. He would read circulars about forthcoming books and then write to the authors asking them why they weren't publishing with Pergamon. He often used to cut through the inertia by looking at problems from a new angle.

'Every publisher has a Permissions Department to which authors or other publishers can write to ask to use a picture or a paragraph of a work published by the firm. The Permissions Department looks up the work in question, checks the copyright and writes back giving permission. Maxwell decided we didn't need a Permissions Department at Pergamon. Many of the senior executives protested: they thought it would be impossible to get by without it. Maxwell said that in future we, the publishing managers, would grant or refuse permission.

'"All we have to do is send the request back with a stamp on it saying: 'Permission granted, on receipt of £20'," he said. "Either they will pay or they won't. There is therefore no need for a filing system to keep copies of responses. If they pay – fine. If they don't – well, we are no worse off. We weren't getting anything in the first place, and anyway we always have the option of suing them in the future."'

Charkin worked for Maxwell for about a year. He discovered that it was time to move on after an interview with the Chairman.

'I was in the National Union of Journalists and had been Father of the Chapel. One day I was called in to see the Chairman. He told me I had a bright future in publishing: "But, Richard, it doesn't sit well with your being a member of a union."

'I was a bit gob-smacked because he was a prospective parliamentary candidate for the Labour Party at the time. I thought the union should kick up a fuss about this, but was told that it wouldn't. Anyway the trade magazine the *Bookseller* used to circulate, as it does in every publishing house. But there was a difference at Pergamon. All the job advertisements at the back of the magazine used to be torn out before it was sent around; Maxwell used to employ someone specially to do this. So when that person came up to me shortly after my interview with the Chairman and pointed out a job he thought I was well suited to at Oxford

University Press, I thought it was time to move on. I got the job, though I had to take a salary cut.'

It was said that Maxwell used to fiddle the royalties he paid to authors. He would get the book in which prospective royalty payments were noted down and would run through them, cutting payments to some authors whose work he didn't like and giving more to other authors. The book always balanced, so that Pergamon didn't save any money. But it was another exhibition of Maxwell's power to give to those he liked and take from those he didn't. As far as he was concerned, rules were there to be broken.

Charkin remembers Maxwell coming in one day with an invoice for 10 copies of a particular book from a retailer. The total was £150.

'He said to us: "Can any of you clever people tell me how to make that £300?"

'There was silence.

'"Right, I will show you how to do it. At the moment we charge in pounds. From today all our invoices will be in dollars at an exchange rate more favourable to us than at the banks."

'"But," we protested, "British booksellers pay in sterling not in dollars."

'"F... them," he said. "And what we sell aren't books, they are journals so we will only give them a 10 per cent discount, not a discount of 35 per cent. That's how to turn £150 into £300."

'And, by and large, it worked!'

* * *

Pergamon was Maxwell's main book-publishing vehicle; and though it is easy to remember the scandals, many who worked for Maxwell during those early years praise the innovations he introduced. Maxwell was the first publisher to use word processors on any scale, and he was one of the first to develop a publishing data base on computer files. He insisted on seeing all mail that came into the company, saying 'every letter is a potential profit opportunity'. He abolished obsolete departments which other publishers kept going and, most important of all, he championed the cause of scientific publishing.

One top publisher today says that what Maxwell did was to 'make publishers realize that they were not selling pages and print – in those days the price of books was simply a matter of how big the book was and how much print it had in it. He made us realize that what we were really selling was information, and that people didn't really care what it was packaged in.'

In 1980, when Maxwell took over the beleaguered British Printing Corporation, he also acquired the general publishers Macdonald. Then, in 1984, he realized one of his life's ambitions – to own a newspaper – when he bought the Mirror Group, consisting mainly of the *Daily Mirror*, *Sunday Mirror*, *The People* and the Scottish *Daily Record*. In 1987 Maxwell attempted to launch a '24-hour' newspaper, *The London Daily News*, with morning and evening editions, but had to close it within five months.

In 1989 he was involved in the publishing deals that finally tipped the empire into bankruptcy when he bought the giant US book publishers Macmillan and the Official Airline Guide. The next year he launched *The European*, the London-produced paper aimed at English-speaking readers throughout Europe. Finally, in March 1991 he made his last publishing acquisition, taking over the New York *Daily News*. (It is untrue to say he bought the paper: its owners, the Chicago Tribune Group, were so desperate to get rid of it that they paid Maxwell to take it off their hands.)

Maxwell's media empire, then, began as both a publishing and a printing operation. But in 1987 Maxwell sold BPC to its management, declaring that he wished to concentrate on publishing. His deals in the United States were part of a master plan, but the plan backfired and despite the sale even of such core companies as Pergamon, it became increasingly obvious to Maxwell watchers during 1991 that eventually his debts would bring him crashing down.

In July 1988 Maxwell had raised 2.6 million to buy Macmillan. During that summer of '88, however, the coming storm was still well below the horizon, and Don Fruehling, the President of the Maxwell-Pergamon publishing group, remembers it as an exciting time.

In the middle of the takeover of Macmillan, Robert Maxwell roared into New York City and took over the Presidential Suite at the Waldorf Astoria. He had often stayed at the Waldorf and had instructed his Pergamon loyalists to have the suite permanently wired for at least two fax machines and several telephone lines. Don Fruehling recalls that the week before Maxwell's occupation of the suite, however, President Reagan had stayed in it and secret service agents had swept the suite for bugs, cutting all the telephone and fax lines that had been installed for Mr Maxwell.

'When he arrived, only one phone line was working and of course this sent him into a frenzy. After much work a temporary set of phones was rigged up through a junction box placed in a cupboard.

'I had left the suite, but was then summoned back by Mr Maxwell. As I hung my coat in the closet, I dislodged a hanger, which hit the junction box and knocked out the total telephone system. Of course, all hell broke loose. I was on my hands and knees in the closet trying to fix it when Maxwell came in, screaming "Who knocked out the phones?"

'From my position on the floor I yelled back: "I did, goddam it!" Surprisingly, he calmed down immediately and merely admonished me by saying: "I know you didn't do it on purpose, but be more careful in the future."'

*　　*　　*

Robert Maxwell was a driven man: many of those who knew him say they've never seen anyone work harder. He hardly seemed to sleep, and he was capable of making deals in different languages on different phones all at once. He would keep a number of deals up in the air and never seemed to confuse one with another.

One former senior Maxwell executive remembers being present in Maxwell's penthouse apartment in London's Holborn Circus when three separate meetings on totally different topics were being held in two of the large rooms. Maxwell would pass from one meeting to the next to find out what progress was being made and to direct the discussion, taking decisions where necessary. By all accounts it was just like a chess grandmaster taking on a number of lesser opponents.

If Maxwell was hard on himself, he was just as hard on his two sons, Ian and Kevin. They had joined their father's media empire and certainly didn't have any special privileges because they were Robert Maxwell's boys. Indeed Maxwell once sacked Ian for failing to meet him at the airport because he preferred the company of a girlfriend. Many people testify to just how harshly Maxwell could treat his sons. Bridget Rowe, Editor of the *Sunday Mirror*, remembers visiting Maxwell one Saturday afternoon to discuss advertising for the paper.

'Robert Maxwell sat at a tiny desk piled high with cheese on toast, bowls of chicken soup, crisps and chocolate bars. Kevin stood at his father's shoulder. I told Maxwell I thought the advertising should be done in the same way as the last campaign. That was very ...

'Maxwell interrupted and said: "No, no, no, no. We must do it with more impact. Hm. Impact. Let's see what Kevin thinks." Kevin cleared his throat but said nothing.

'Maxwell said: "Well, can my son speak?" Still Kevin said nothing. I was very embarrassed, and started to say that it was very difficult for Kevin because he didn't know ... Maxwell brusquely interrupted me: "What do you mean, he doesn't know? He's a f.....g director of Maxwell Communication Corporation."

'I started to try and explain but was again interrupted. Maxwell said: "Let him speak for himself."

'There was a pause, then his father looked at Kevin and said: "Well?"

'Kevin said nothing. Maxwell said: "The trouble with him is that he never ate his beans as a child." This made me even more embarrassed, but I felt I had to say something: "Er ... you don't like baked beans, Kevin?" Again Kevin made no attempt to answer.

'His father said: "No, he didn't like baked beans. He didn't like runner beans. He didn't like broad beans. Look at him! Go away, go away and eat some beans!" Still without saying a word, Kevin walked out of the room and shut the door behind him.'

*   *   *

In the mid-1980s a consortium of publishers was formed to invest in electronic publishing. The new company was called Adonis, and Pergamon, Blackwell Scientific, Elsevier from Holland and Springer from Germany were the publishers involved. Robert Campbell, who is now Managing Director of Blackwell Scientific Publishing, was in charge of his company's interest in the new firm.

'I chaired a meeting in Frankfurt the day before the International Book Fair. Robert Maxwell attended, along with two distinguished colleagues from Germany and Holland. We were discussing whether or not to go ahead with a certain project, and I commented that we could not stall for much longer and that we were beginning to look like paper tigers. Maxwell agreed vehemently, paused, then said that he was not going to have anyone call him a wanker. Having established our position, I attempted to move on, but I was interrupted by our German colleague.

'"Excuse me, vot is a vanker?"

'I indicated to Maxwell that he might handle this one. After a moment's thought, he explained that it was a "derogatory term". This seemed good enough to me, so I tried to move on again – but no: "If somebody calls me a vanker I vish to know vot a vanker is."

'I felt that, as Maxwell had introduced the term, it was up to him to explain it. He was not happy, but after an uncomfortable silence he declared:

"A wanker is a chap that does it with two hands in front of a mirror."

*   *   *

Per Saugman, a Director of Blackwell Scientific, recalls a sequel to one of the many tussles his company had with Maxwell.

'Some years ago we were in competition with Pergamon Press concerning an international journal, and we won the contract. Robert Maxwell rang to offer his congratulations and to say it had been a fair fight. He invited me to his office at Headington Hill Hall on the following Sunday at 9 am to discuss one or two matters.

'After several security bells had been pushed I was ushered into Maxwell's office. He offered me some coffee, but first filled his own cup, which was practically the size of a soup bowl and had written on the inside in inch tall gold letters: "God bless our father."

'After he had filled his cup there was not a drop of coffee left in the pot. He pressed a variety of buttons on the coffee machine, all to no avail, and declared with a sigh that he could not seem to get any reaction. I suggested to him, tongue in cheek, that perhaps it was easier to telephone Tokyo judging by the enormous map in the building which detailed all the links in the Pergamon empire. He then pushed a very large mahogany cigar case across the table at me and offered me a cigar. When he opened the case there was one lonely cigar lying at the bottom. I told him that his need was probably greater than mine and that I had in any case brought my own. They were, curiously enough, the same make as his – Davidoff!

'After a moment's silence, he demanded \$100,000 for

Pergamon's subscription list. I told him we had no intention of paying for a list he had been given for nothing. Trying another tack, he said that if I had worked for him I would be a rich man. I told him I was adequately wealthy already!

'When I left Maxwell's office 11 people were queuing up to get an interview. That was the end of a most extraordinary Sunday morning.'

*   *   *

Ken Hudgell was Company Secretary of the Mirror Group for 20 years. He describes Maxwell's time in charge as the most unhappy period of his life.

'I was working one day in my office, sitting at my desk, tearing up a piece of paper, when Robert Maxwell walked in. He shouted: "Stop! You are destroying company property." I told him it was a change of address card and that I had already noted the new address.

'This was shortly after Maxwell had "rescued" the *Daily Mirror* and he said: "Don't do anything without asking my permission. When will you *Mirror* people ever learn? That's my chair you're sitting on, my desk and my carpet you've got your feet on – and don't you ever forget it."

'I remember an occasion in the early 1980s when we were meeting the union representatives at the Mirror Group – the Fathers of the Chapels. They were unhappy about the returns on the pension fund investments. There was some argument between Bob Maxwell and the unions about whose money was in the pension funds.

'Robert Maxwell said: "The money is mine." The union representatives asked how that could possibly be true since he had only recently taken over the group.

'He turned to me and said: "We'll ask the company secretary, Ken Hudgell."

'I said, "The assets are held by a trustee company on behalf of Mirror Group Newspapers and the Scottish *Daily Record*."

'"And who owns them?" he demanded.

"'Pergamon Press."

"'And who owns Pergamon Press?"

'I said it was owned by a Maxwell family trust based in Liechtenstein.

"'And who owns that?"

"'Well, you do, I suppose."

"'So," Maxwell said triumphantly, "I own the pension funds.'"

*   *   *

In 1985 Harry Templeton was appointed a trustee of the Mirror Group Pension scheme. He left three years later after being sacked for 'gross industrial misconduct', but Mr Templeton says he was really dismissed simply to remove him from the board of trustees. Before the House of Commons Social Security Select Committee in February 1992 he outlined how he had joined the board of trustees against the wishes of Robert Maxwell, and the lengths to which Mr Maxwell was prepared to go to in an attempt to intimidate him.

Mr Templeton said: 'I worked as a printer on the Scottish *Daily Record* and the *Sunday Mail* and had been the union official not only for the printers but for the whole building. I was called an imperial father, like a senior shop steward. We had a representative on the board of trustees and we had become worried that the board did not seem to be doing much so far as we were concerned. The source of our concern, within the plant, was that we distrusted Robert Maxwell and we were anxious to protect our pensions. So we decided to hold an election. As a result of that election I was voted to replace the existing trustee for Scotland as the worker-appointed trustee. Maxwell refused to accept my appointment. At one point he said I would get on to the board of trustees over his dead body. That was the first time I realized he was not a man to be trusted, because when I got on he lived on!'

At this point Harry Templeton's narrative was interrupted

by the committee chairman, Frank Field, MP, who said: 'Only for a time, Mr Templeton.'

Templeton responded 'Yes, only for a time.' Then he went on to outline Robert Maxwell's opposition to him as a pension-board trustee.

'He tried everything to prevent me getting on to the board. The workers on the *Record* had to write individually, giving their membership number. Hundreds of letters were sent, insisting Maxwell accept my appointment to the board. When ultimately I got on to the board he refused to allow me to attend the first meeting: he said they could accept new members to the board only at the end of the first day's business. ... He was not at all keen to have me as a trustee.'

On another occasion Maxwell made it clear to Templeton that he regarded the pension fund as his. Templeton told the select committee that he had questioned why Maxwell had so much control over the pension fund. After all, when Maxwell bought the group he paid £113 million for it. At the time there was about £350 million in the pension fund. Maxwell made contributions on behalf of the company of about a million pounds a month for about nine months. Templeton's view was that the rest of the money was the workers' and the former employees'. Since he, Maxwell, had put so little in, why should he have so much control?

Templeton said: 'He would say: "I will tell you why I have so much control. When I bought the company, I bought the pension fund. If there is a shortfall in the pension fund they will not come to you asking you to make it good, they will come to me. I am the person who has to make good any shortfall in the pension fund. Do not tell me it is your pension fund! It is my pension fund."

'He said it was his fund, his money. If I questioned the surplus he would say: "Do not push me too far on the surplus; if you do I will wind up the fund. You will get your entitlement but I will laugh all the way to the bank."'

*   *   *

Maxwell's clashes with the unions became legendary. Although his arch-rival, Rupert Murdoch, is often credited with breaking the stranglehold of the print unions in Fleet Street by locking them out from his works at Wapping, where *The Times* and *Sunday Times* are printed, it was Maxwell and his earlier victories that made that possible.

In 1981 Maxwell was asked to take control of the British Printing Corporation, the biggest company of its kind in the UK. National Westminster Bank was behind the invitation because it was owed £25 million by BPC. The corporation was horrendously overmanned; it was inefficient and many of its 42 trading companies were making heavy losses.

The feeling in the City was that only Maxwell could take on the unions, reorganize the group and make the redundancies necessary to put the company back in profit.

In many of BPC's factories it was accepted that there had to be change. But at the Park Royal printing works there was fierce resistance. Park Royal was a purpose-built West London factory where the principal activity was to print Britain's biggest-selling magazine, *Radio Times*. As *Radio Times'* circulation increased it became necessary to print copies at a second plant (at East Kilbride). Printing at Park Royal was very expensive for two reasons: one was that it was still done on outdated hot-metal presses; the other was that its print union members came under the Central London branch of SOGAT '82. As such they were very highly paid – on the same scale as their colleagues in Fleet Street – and they had the backing of an extremely powerful union branch.

Maxwell wanted to cut the number of Park Royal employees and change working practices in order to stem the £2 million a year loss he said was being made on printing the magazine. Over a three-year period there were a number of confrontations, culminating in the events of autumn 1983. The union said it would fight Maxwell's proposal to close the plant, and in November Maxwell issued to workers what he called a 'one-last-chance' letter demanding total participation in the production of the Christmas issue of

Radio Times. Five days later he said the Park Royal plant would close with the loss of 400 jobs. On 13 November engineers moved into Park Royal to dismantle the printing presses.

John Mitchell, formerly secretary of SOGAT's London machine room branch, recalls: 'They smashed them up using 14lb hammers. Maxwell told us the machines were old anyway and that he would replace them with modern web-offset presses – provided the SOGAT machine assistants would operate five-day rather than four-day working.

'I commented to the papers that this was the first set of negotiations I had attended with 14lb hammers being one of the bargaining points. The remark found its way into the "Sayings of the Week" column in the *Observer* I received a call at 8am Sunday morning from Robert Maxwell congratulating me on my witty remark and on having "arrived" on the national scene. He seemed to find it very amusing and seemed as pleased with himself as if he'd said it.

'After one round of arduous union talks the meeting broke up and Maxwell asked Fred Smith if he would like a lift to the railway station. [Smith is retired now but was then a national negotiator who'd known Maxwell for some years.] As they were driving along in the chauffeur-driven Rolls Royce, Maxwell suddenly turned to Fred and said: "Do you fancy something to eat?" This was an open invitation to Fred who was himself quite a large man and fond of his food. He was aware of Maxwell's reputation as a gourmet so he thought that if Maxwell had invited him to eat the food might be worth having.

'Maxwell asked his driver to pull over. He went into a hamburger joint, and came out with a parcel. Fred was not unnaturally a little disappointed. But he was also hungry. Maxwell had bought six portions of hamburger and chips. He ate four of them and Fred had to make do with two!'

A similar fate befell one Deputy Editor of the *Daily Mirror* while travelling with Maxwell in his Rolls Royce. Suddenly Maxwell announced: 'I'm hungry!' and told the driver to stop at a fish and chip shop he'd spotted. He got out of the car and returned with two portions of fish and chips. He ate both packets, refraining from offering a single chip to the man sitting beside him.

By the time he had finished his snack, the car was travelling along the M25. Maxwell threw the wrapping paper out of the car. Unfortunately it hit the windscreen of a police car. The Rolls was signalled to stop and a policeman appeared at Maxwell's window. The officer cautioned Maxwell about the dangers of throwing rubbish on to the motorway. Maxwell asked the policeman if he realized who he was talking to.

'I am Robert Maxwell, the owner of the *Daily Mirror*.'

The officer told him he didn't care who he was and that what he had done could have been very dangerous.

'I quite realize that,' said Maxwell. 'Indeed, I told him not to do it,' he added, pointing to the unfortunate Deputy Editor. 'I can assure you that he will be severely reprimanded, and may even lose his job!'

* * *

Bob Cole, as we have seen, was Press Officer of Maxwell Communications Corporation for many years. He recalls an early brush with the tycoon.

'I joined the British Printing Corporation (BPC) in 1962, and I came across Maxwell a few times in the 1960s. When he took over at BPC I was manager of Print House, the company headquarters. I looked after the staff, security, the office budget, stationery and that sort of thing.

'Maxwell was a very big man and I remember seeing him arrive for his very first BPC board meeting. Shortly afterwards he called on me. He told me he wanted a room cleared and a bed put in. There were also to be coffee making facilities.

'He said: "If I'm going to save this organization, I'm going to have to sleep here." There was nothing unusual in this, he always lived above the shop. He always had a large office and he always had managers sitting outside waiting to see him: they were just like patients waiting to see the doctor.

'Now, a few days after I'd set up a room where he could sleep, I was passing the Chairman's office when he came out and shouted "Mister!" I turned to see who he was talking to and realized it was me.

'He said: "You nearly lost 18,000 people their jobs last night!" I thought I must have left the office safe open or contributed to some other financial disaster.

'Maxwell continued: "My room was freezing cold last night. If I had caught pneumonia and died it would have been down to you. Without me this corporation would be doomed to failure and the consequence of that would be that 18,000 people would lose their jobs."

'"But, Mr Maxwell," I protested, "there was an electric fire in the room."

'"But did it have a label on it with instructions on how to switch it on?"

'"No," I admitted.

'Maxwell looked straight at me and said: "Well, by great good fortune I didn't catch pneumonia so 18,000 jobs have been saved. But it's no thanks to you!"'

*   *   *

At the beginning of the 1980s Eddie Coffey ran Hodder & Stoughton in Australia. He met Maxwell while he was on a business trip to Britain, and was invited to come and see him at Headington Hill Hall. Maxwell was with his sales director when Coffey was shown in to his office. Maxwell asked the sales director if he thought they should ask Coffey to represent their interests in Australia. The sales director replied honestly, saying that he felt they should not because they were already adequately served there. Maxwell then turned to Coffey and said that the sales director's opinion didn't matter anyway, that *he* gave the orders at Pergamon and that he'd already decided to ask Coffey to act for them.

Some years later, in 1986, Coffey was in London and was asked to visit Maxwell at his office in Holborn Circus. 'I remember it was the day of his libel case at the Old Bailey. I was due to see him at 3.30 so I had arrived at a quarter past, but by 3.45 I hadn't managed to get in to see him. I told his secretary that I had to go soon, and then I was ushered into the presence.

'He asked me to sit down and I said I would prefer to stand. He then offered me a job as a publishing director with a salary of £100,000 a year.

'I turned him down. He accepted that, but then said: "Can you help me buy Hodder & Stoughton?"

'I told him I was too old for that sort of work, and he said: "If you help me make this acquisition I will pay you a million pounds."

'Again I turned him down. Finally he offered me £50,000 a year to run his publishing interests in Australia and New Zealand. Once more I declined his offer.

'Then he asked me if I could help him buy an Australian newspaper. He said the *Melbourne Age* attracted him, but he wanted to know what I thought of the Australian press. I said I thought it was awful. And that was the end of our conversation. I never joined Maxwell because ever since the early 1970s I had gained the impression that the way he generated profits was to over-value stocks; and although he was always very kind to me I never really trusted him enough to work for him.'

*   *   *

When Maxwell bought Mirror Group Newspapers the Labour Party seemed to favour his takeover because at least he had pledged that he would keep the *Daily Mirror* a Labour-supporting paper. Since the rest of the popular press in Fleet Street supported the Tories, this was not an insignificant matter.

However, many people expressed fears at the time that his ownership would lead to a fearsome confrontation with the unions. The National Union of Journalists and the print union, SOGAT '82, announced that they were 'totally opposed' to Maxwell or any other individual taking over the Mirror Group.

For a time all was well. But eventually the showdown between Maxwell and the unions took place over one of the group's lesser known titles, *The Sporting Life*. In August 1985 Maxwell decided to typeset the paper outside London in an attempt to cut down its losses.

One of the two main print unions, the National Graphical Association (NGA), immediately instructed its branches outside London not to negotiate with Maxwell. There was disruption of the *Daily Mirror* by the unions and 750,000 copies of the paper were lost. Maxwell tried to obtain a promise from the NGA that it would not act in the same way again, but he failed; he then announced that 300 NGA members had 'dismissed themselves'.

Maxwell used his papers in Scotland to argue his case. In the *Sunday Mail*, which was unaffected by the action, he said that *The Sporting Life* was losing a pound a week for every reader it had. At the height of the dispute he brought out an emergency issue of the paper which was produced so cheaply he could give it away to its main customers, the bookmakers. However, as Bob Cole remembers, Maxwell went to even greater lengths for one prestigious racing enthusiast.

'We had heard that the Queen was furious if she didn't get her copy of *The Sporting Life*. So for the duration of the strike Maxwell undertook to produce one copy of the paper for Her Majesty every day, and he said he wanted me to deliver it to the palace personally. I said that wouldn't be a problem. But what we had overlooked was that it was summertime and the Queen was resident at Balmoral, her estate in the Scottish highlands.

'So Maxwell arranged for me to fly up to Aberdeen every day and then to connect with a helicopter to take me to Balmoral just so I could deliver Her Majesty's copy of

Sporting Life. During the period of these daily flights, Maxwell said to me: "If you get an OBE for this – it's mine!'"

*   *   *

When Maxwell took over Mirror Group Newspapers he began to weed out bad practices – among them inflated expenses claims by journalists. It was said that in many desk drawers there were bottles of spirits which had been bought on expenses, and Maxwell decreed that this was now forbidden. For a time everyone was too terrified of upsetting the new boss to do anything else. Then one day one of the journalists decided to revive the glorious tradition of the 'bottle on expenses'. For a couple of weeks, nothing was said. Then one Sunday afternoon he received a phone call from 'The Publisher', who asked to see him in his holy of holies on the 10th floor. When the worried scribbler appeared, Maxwell was watching television. He told his visitor to sit down and asked him if he liked whisky. The journalist was resigning himself to a tirade, when Maxwell explained that he had invited him up 'because you seem to be the only one in the newsroom who drinks'. It turned out that Maxwell was simply a little lonely and wanted someone to watch the live football on television with him.

*   *   *

In the early part of 1991 Robert Maxwell focused his attention on the New York *Daily News*. The paper had just the right ingredients for a succesful Maxwell rescue recipe: yit was losing money hand over fist; had terrible problems with the unions; and had been disrupted by industrial action of one sort or another over the past two years. The paper was suffering from the sort of problems that had been sorted out by Maxwell and Murdoch in Fleet Street – overmanning, restrictive practices, antiquated machinery and uncontrolled expenditure. The owners, the Chicago Tribune Group, could see no way of ridding themselves of their obligations. According to them the newspaper's accumulated losses since 1980 were $250 million: it was losing $700,000 a week. They had threatened to close the paper down by 14 March unless a buyer could be found. Enter Maxwell. He knew how to appeal to everyone.

One of the key union negotiators was George Macdonald, President of the Allied Printing Trades Council: 'When we knew Maxwell was interested in buying the *News* I phoned some British trade unionists and they warned me to "watch him". But when he came over we got into a pretty good relationship. We found out we had a lot in common. We were both born under the same birth sign, Gemini, and within 10 days of each other: he was 10 days older than me. But he was 6ft 3in tall and weighed about 400lb: I was 5ft 8in and weighed about 155!

'Now, at the time a movie had just been released over here in the States called *Twins*, starring Arnold Schwarzenegger and Danny DeVito. Arnold is, as you know, a pretty large guy but Danny is only 5ft tall. It kind of became a joke between us. Maxwell would say, "Where is my twin?" when he was referring to me. It was that sort of lighthearted talk that helped him win the unions over to his rescue package.'

Ted Khell was an adviser to the unions during the negotiations for the sale of the *Daily News* to Maxwell. He was in a unique position to observe how Maxwell operated.

'He arrived on the scene to begin negotiating with 10 unions for the takeover of the *News*. In the newspaper industry here, all 10 unions are independent but at the same time totally dependent on each other. It had been the practice here that, during negotiations, the parties rented space in hotels where they could carry on 24-hour talks if need be and have the luxury of room service.

'During Rupert Murdoch's talks to take over the New York *Post* in 1988 meetings had taken place at the Hyatt Regency. Maxwell announced that the two sides were to meet in the offices of his company Macmillan Inc. on 3rd

Avenue. There were a number of floors vacant in the building and Maxwell arranged for the unions to have rooms on one floor, for him to have rooms on another floor and for a third floor to be kept for meetings between the two sides.

'He had the offices furnished with rented furniture and arranged for room service throughout the day and night with a deli and a Chinese restaurant nearby. During the "10 days that shook New York" I remember thinking that I had never seen so much food in my life. In the morning we would come in and there would be piles of danish pastries, muffins, coffee and orange juice. All day long there would be a steady stream of waiters bringing in food from the deli and the Chinese restaurant. The unions loved him for this because he told everyone he would pick up the tab.

'On day one there was a general meeting of all the unions. The President of the most important of them, Mike Alvina of the Drivers' Union, was late. (In the newspaper industry in America today it is no longer possible to stop a paper printing but it is still possible to stop it being delivered – hence the critical importance of the Drivers' Union.) Now, Mike Alvina was always late. It was well known in the unions that he habitually excused himself by explaining that he'd been "stuck in traffic in a tunnel".

'Anyway, at this particular meeting everyone was assembled, Maxwell was there, but there was no sign of Alvina.

'Eventually he turned up. Maxwell looked at him and said: "Oh, Lord Alvino, thank you for coming." Mike smiled – he was kind of flattered and enjoyed telling his family about it. Throughout the negotiations he was addressed by Maxwell as "Lord Alvino". In small ways like this he created an atmosphere to his advantage.'

(In fact, it's more likely that Maxwell was referring to Mike Alvina as 'Lord Elvino' after El Vino's, the famous Fleet Street watering hole.)

Maxwell's success as a negotiator was, of course, more securely based than merely knowing how to flatter people.

He seemed to know instinctively what people wanted to hear. He was also a good orator. In America the unions, particularly in the newspaper business, have found themselves under the sort of pressure that their counterparts in Britain faced in the early 1980s. Maxwell knew just how to play this card, as Ted Khell describes.

'Virtually the first thing Robert Maxwell did was to make a speech to the unions. He was utterly charming. He condemned the tactics which the former owners, the Chicago Tribune Group, had employed. They had hired 800 replacements for the striking employees and told them they would be permanent replacements. Under the United States law as laid down by the Supreme Court in 1938 a company could replace striking workers and agree to keep those replacements on after the strike ended. This legislation had been little used until the 1980s, when lots of employers seemed to want to use it as a cudgel to bash the unions. But it was counterproductive: if you knew even if the strike ended that you weren't going to get your job back, then what did you have to lose?

'This attitude by employers led union members to resort to violence and during the strike at the New York *Daily News*, trucks had been burned and newsstands torched. Maxwell promised everyone from the outset that with an agreement all those workers who had been on strike would get their old jobs back and that the 800 people who'd been employed as replacements would be sent packing. This was one of the main items that the unions had in fact been fighting for with the Chicago Tribune Group.

'Then Maxwell told us all a little about himself and his history. He described how he grew up in Czechoslovakia, how he had fought during the Second World War and how he had eventually settled in England. He told us he had at one time had a choice and could have come to America but decided to go to England. He said, though, that he often reflected on his choice and wondered what would have happened had he come to the United States. He said he had

a great affection for America but that he was a loyal subject
of Her Majesty the Queen. He added here that he was unlike
another publisher who had given up his citizenship in order
to take over a television network. He never mentioned Rupert
Murdoch by name, but we all knew who he was talking
about.

'He stressed how he had been a Labour MP and a
supporter of the Labour movement all his life. How he
believed in unions and wanted to reach an agreement but
that any agreement must include that there should be an end
to unnecessary overtime and that any overtime had to be
approved by him personally. He told us he was going to
remain in the United States for six months to sort out the
paper. In fact he only stayed six days. He had other problems
elsewhere to sort out.

'On the first day under Maxwell, the paper ran into
overtime while printing. It was delivered in the suburbs but
not in the city. In view of what Maxwell had said at the
meeting, no one wanted to take responsibility for the overtime payments. They hunted for him everywhere but
without success. In the end they decided to shut down the
presses. So hardly anyone in New York got the paper that
day.'

*   *   *

As Maxwell's Press Officer, Bob Cole was used to working
unsocial hours: 'I was at home asleep when the phone rang.
The voice on the other end said: "This is Dover Police." (I
don't recall his name but it was a fairly high-ranking officer.)
He went on: "I think you should know that the last time
this country was invaded was by William the Conqueror.
Well, I believe that Mr Maxwell now holds the new record because he is the cause of the second invasion of this
island."

'I asked him what was going on and what it had to do
with Mr Maxwell. He said: "Do you know of a company
called Imprenorne Française?"

'I said that I did. He asked me if there was a dispute there. I said there was.

'He said: "Well you are not going to believe this, but the French strikers have managed to get access to the Channel Tunnel and are half way across the Straits of Dover!"

'As it later turned out, the strikers' plan to invade Britain over their dispute with Robert Maxwell had been thwarted because an airlock on the British side of the Channel Tunnel had been secured and they were unable to get through. When I phoned Maxwell he thought the whole thing was hilarious, but that nevertheless he would phone the Home Secretary and ask for the army to be put on standby. In the end the French strikers were forced to take the Hovercraft over and later they picketed the Mirror building.

'I received another call in the middle of the night only last year. I thought it was so urgent that I phoned Mr Maxwell straight away. He was asleep, but eventually answered the phone himself.

'I said: "It's Bob Cole, Mr Maxwell."

'He responded by saying: "I know that, you pratt. This had better be good!"

'I said: "Mr Maxwell, I think you should know there has been a coup in Russia. It would seem that Mr Gorbachev has been deposed whilst he was in his holiday home in the Crimea. The whole place seems to be in turmoil."

'Maxwell said simply: "Very well, leave it to me."

'I understand that he then rang Prime Minister John Major, spoke to the Russian Ambassador and telephoned Boris Yeltsin (he actually had Yeltsin's home number!). I am sure that Mr Maxwell and I were among the first half a dozen people in Britain to know about the coup.

'As a postscript to this story, I was walking down Bromley High Street doing some early morning shopping when my mobile phone rang. It was, of course, Robert Maxwell. The traffic was so noisy that I couldn't hear him so I went into a department store and stood by one of the counters.

'He wanted me to take down a statement to be released to all newspaper editors. It outlined how, following the coup in the Soviet Union, he had been able to contact the Prime Minister, John Major, earlier that morning. The statement went on that he had put Mr Major in touch with the Russian leader, Boris Yeltsin, and that he felt proud to have played a part in the successful outcome of the coup, which had resulted in Mr Gorbachev being freed.

'I was trying to write this down while at the same time holding the phone to my ear in the middle of a busy department store. Every so often the girl on the till would give me a strange look. I'm convinced she thought I was mad.'

Bob Cole was Robert Maxwell's Press Officer for 10 years. Maxwell would insist on having full editorial control over what was sent out in his name. If Cole suggested too many alterations Maxwell would cut off any argument by saying: 'Mister, you are my postman, not my censor.' But Maxwell did not hesitate to impose censorship on his own editors. Roy Greenslade, former Editor of the *Daily Mirror*:

'On 13 January Gorbachev sent Soviet tanks into Vilnius, capital of Lithuania, in a bid to quell the growing movement for independence. Several people were killed, and pictures showed troops acting with undue severity against protestors and the press. With Maxwell on his way to New York the leader writer, David Thompson, and I were in a position to assess the situation ourselves. His excellent leader pointed out that the Soviet president was either a liar, having promised not to take military action, or had lost control of the army.

'When Maxwell arrived in his hotel to read the faxed letter he exploded. Thompson got the first call, Maxwell describing his leader as "immature" and "politically naive". He demanded that it be rewritten to point out that the Lithuanians had brought all this on themselves by refusing to let their young men be conscripted into the army. Regrettable though the deaths were it was their own fault for making a "direct threat to Soviet authority". Inconsequentially, he ended by suggesting that if the Lithuanians wanted independence they should negotiate it with Gorbachev.

'A reluctant Thompson was forced to comply unless I could change Maxwell's mind and we both doubted that were possible. When I spoke to him Maxwell said: "Why have I received this disgraceful leader?"

"'Bob," I said, "the pictures of violence are horrific. What appears to be happening is a virtual invasion of the country."

'Before I could continue he shouted: "We must not abandon Gorbachev. I will decide." I tried to explain, as so often in the past, that news was news. The journalists on the *Mirror* and the independent agencies were reporting what was happening.

'He interrupted, and his tone was at its most menacing: "Look, mister, you are talking nonsense. Don't you realize that Gorbachev wouldn't do anything without ringing me first?"'

*   *   *

Roy Greenslade wasn't the only editor to have trouble with Maxwell over matters Soviet. Bridget Rowe, the Editor of the *Sunday Mirror*, had similar problems.

'The most memorable time for me was the Saturday when everything was going particularly wrong for Gorbachev. There was absolute chaos in Russia. Gorbachev was about to disappear down to that house by the lake [his holiday home in the Crimea] and Maxwell was in France.

'Now, before I joined the *Sunday Mirror* I had come to a deal with Maxwell. I knew his reputation for fiddling and meddling with the newspapers he owned and I really didn't want to be there as Deputy Editor, so we had an agreement that the only thing he had a major say in was the leader. He kept pretty well to that deal but on this particular Saturday it caused absolute chaos because there was a planned leader which was to be very supportive of Gorbachev. Then it came over the wires, on CNN and on the news, that it was the end for Gorbachev.

'So I phoned Maxwell in France and said: "Right, we are changing the leader. Gorbachev is on the way out."

'Maxwell said: "Don't be ridiculous!"

'I said: "It is the end."

'Maxwell countered with: "You've all gone mad. Who told you this?"

'I said: "It's even on the BBC."

'"BBC?" he said. "They don't know anything about things like this. Phone my friend in Russia." He gave me a phone number and added: "Speak to him in Russian."

'I said: "I don't speak Russian."

'He exploded and said: "Oh, I don't know why I've got you there, you can't speak Russian. I'll have to do it myself. I have to do everything myself."

'In a little while he phoned back and said: "My friend wasn't in. If there had been a problem my friend would have been in, so there is no problem with Gorbachev at all."

'As the afternoon went on, I thought: "This is ridiculous." And so we changed the leader and there was much fighting, rowing and screaming from France. If Maxwell got something into his head, wild Shetland ponies couldn't persuade him that it was far from the truth.

'A few Saturdays later someone was trying to serve an injunction on us and we had to go in front of a judge. Maxwell always used to say: "Oh, for God's sake, how did you get us into this mess this morning?" True to form, he said it this Saturday. I told him not to worry and that we would have any injunction against us lifted.

'Maxwell then said: "Money, money, money, lawyers and barristers. I suppose you want everybody – George Carman QC – in there as well? Oh, come upstairs and show me everything. I'm the chief litigator around here."

'I went upstairs and Maxwell had two German friends with him. He said: "Come and meet my friends and speak to them in German."

'I said: "I don't speak German."'

'He exploded. "I don't f....g believe this. You don't speak Russian and now you tell me you don't speak German. She doesn't speak German!" Of course, these German guys spoke English. But Maxwell had this thing about languages. I heard him speak French, Russian, German, Italian and a bit of Japanese.'

* * *

Robert Maxwell was usually very well informed about foreign affairs, but that didn't stop him making mistakes. On one occasion during the abortive Soviet coup against Mikhail Gorbachev, he rang the news desk of the *Daily Mirror* and said: 'I have phoned to tell you that Boris Yeltsin is dead. He's been shot.' The anonymous journalist in the newsroom replied that he didn't think that was so.

Maxwell said: 'I'm telling you Boris Yeltsin is dead. What makes you doubt what I'm saying?' The voice in the newsroom said: 'Because I am watching Mr Yeltsin live on CNN Television. He's standing on a tank. I do not think he could do that if he was dead.'

Mr Maxwell's response is not recorded.

* * *

Maxwell was often accused of 'sucking up' to the Communist leaders of Eastern Europe. He came to regard Mikhail Gorbachev as some sort of super-hero. So much so that, according to Sir Bernard Audley, he was willing to make an exhibition of himself!

'He decided – like all his decisions, shooting from the hip – to have a Perestroika exhibition in the *Daily Mirror* building. This was to have been attended initially by Gorbachev. In the end it was the second in command in the Politburo who attended.

'There were various exhibits, but pride of place was given to a 50-ton Joseph Stalin tank, which was shunted up onto the fourth floor of the Mirror Building. Horror upon

horrors – the floor began to sag and it became clear it was
going to crash four floors into the Mirror basement. But by
that time our hero was probably in his helicopter winging
his way somewhere, and the damage was left to other people
to clear up. I'm not certain but I think they sent for the
fire brigade to shore it up. The exhibition itself was a
disaster. But it fulfilled a purpose – on to the next water
lily.'

*   *   *

Maxwell used to hold regular Tuesday lunches for all
the editors in Mirror Group Newspapers – even those
from Scotland had to travel down to Maxwell's offices
in Holborn. The food, according to Roy Greenslade,
was often bland and meagre. Maxwell drank wine from
his own bottle while the others were all given inferior
plonk. Maxwell's unpredictability meant that lunches
were often cancelled at short notice or started very late.
After a succession of delayed starts over a number of
weeks, Roy Greenslade turned up to find that Maxwell
had arrived on time and that he had ordered lunch to
begin.

Maxwell looked at Greenslade and boomed: 'Why are you
late, Mister Greenslade?'

'I'm sorry, Bob, but I was sorting out an exclusive story,'
replied Greenslade.

Maxwell replied, 'That's not a good enough reason for
being late for me.'

Two minutes later the advertising director, Roger Eastoe,
arrived to a similar growled inquiry.

'I was sealing a deal for a million quid's worth of business,'
he said brightly, expecting a word of praise.

'That's not a reason for being late, Roger the Dodger,'
said Maxwell. 'Don't do it again.'

Some five minutes later still, the then *Sunday Mirror* editor
Eve Pollard turned up and was also called to account.

'I was talking to my daughter,' she said.

'That is family,' said Maxwell. 'Family is the only reason I will accept for lateness at my lunches.'

* * *

Early in 1951 Robert Maxwell was approached to take over book wholesalers Simpkin Marshall. The company was owned by Pitmans, then one of the country's biggest publishers. Simpkin Marshall was a strange British institution, acting as a wholesale intermediary between publishers and the bookshops. Booksellers, many of whom have only one shop, were able to order small quantities of publishers' books through Simpkin Marshall, which kept a central warehouse stocking work from all publishers. Simpkins boasted that it stocked nearly every book in print, together with many long out of print, and that books ordered on the telephone could be delivered the next day. As the bookshops paid the same price for books ordered through Simpkin's as they would had they bought directly from the publisher, Simpkin's made their profits by obtaining the books from the publishers at discount. With an annual turnover of £1 million Simpkin's profits before the war were acceptable. But in December 1940, during one of the worst nights of the Blitz, Simpkin's warehouse was hit by a bomb and four million books were destroyed.

The publishers made a half-hearted attempt to resurrect Simpkin Marshall, but many of them begrudged taking smaller profits than they might make by selling directly to booksellers. Pitmans took on responsibility for Simpkin Marshall, but by 1951 Simpkin's debts had risen to £250,000.

In stepped Maxwell with his usual belief that he could solve the problems of any troubled business. He bought Simpkin Marshall from Pitmans, and then a year later used company money to buy the British Book Center in New York from a Conservative member of Parliament, Captain Peter Baker MC. At the time Maxwell and Baker were very friendly and it has been suggested that Maxwell was sounding out the chances of his standing as a Conservative MP.

Baker's manager at the time was Jimmy Shaw, who's now a sprightly octogenarian living in Scotland.

'One day Peter Baker rang me and said: "I want to introduce you to Captain Robert Maxwell MC." I'm sitting at my desk some time later when a limousine pulls up outside the building. Peter emerges followed by this tall handsome man who turned out to be Robert Maxwell. They came upstairs and I was introduced to Maxwell and he seemed to take to me straight away. He later said he wanted me to work for him and to name my own salary. Anyway, on this occasion he asked me about the business. He had just taken over Simpkin Marshall and was later to buy the British Book Center in New York from Peter.

'Bob Maxwell was a very clever man – an extremely clever man. But in the first half hour of our first meeting he told me the biggest, most blatant lie I ever heard. I had told him we were exporting very well to the Far East and Japan. He said that he too was doing good business throughout the world and then he said: "In fact I am exporting £5,000 worth of books every month to Japan." I knew this to be a lie because at that time there was a strict quota on the amount of books the Japanese could import. This figure was many times the permitted amount. From that date I never really trusted him. I suppose that is why I never went to work for him – probably just as well, really.'

*   *   *

To Robert Maxwell a promise could be used to entice executives to join him and to keep them in place when they did. But just like currency notes, promises tend to be devalued when too many of them are in circulation. Donald Davies had been Chief Executive of the Pitman Group but had joined Robert Maxwell on a promise. He started in BPC in 1980, ostensibly to head up the publishing division, but Maxwell had promised him that he had in mind to appoint a Group Chief Executive and that man was to be Donald Davies.

'Maxwell told me that the business was expanding so much that his own job was getting too much for him to cope with and that is why he wanted to appoint a group chief executive. He said the decision would be announced in June 1982, but that he would offer it to me. It was supposed to be a big job and the person appointed would be a director of 42 companies and chairman of 20. There would be a large salary and a large Mercedes car to go with it.

'I was waiting to see Maxwell one day and began telling one of my colleagues about the promise. He started to smile and said that he thought I should go for a drink with him in a nearby pub after work. This I did and when we were inside he said: "Let me introduce you to all the other Group Chief Executives elect."

'Half the time no one knew what job they were supposed to be doing because Maxwell used to swop everyone around; I was group finance director for a week. Not one of us took it really seriously. We liked to think of ourselves as an escape committee and we used to meet in the pub to discuss ways out of the Maxwell organization. We realized there were only three ways out of what we called Maxwell's Madhouse, the headquarters of BPC in Worship Street in the east end of the City. You could join Maxwell's Moonies and walk around with a glazed look on your face, immune to insults or abuse, simply obeying his orders. You could get the sack, or you could escape under the wire and find a job and resign before he sacked you. That was where the skill came in. If an executive managed to do that he held what was called an "escape party". I managed to hold an "escape party" – but then I had been looking for another job since the day after I joined the organization.

'Working for Maxwell was literally like being in the fabled Colditz. He used to subject people to the sort of psychological pressure that you can imagine the Germans using during the war. If his advisers disagreed with him, he would ring them night after night at three or four o'clock, until they caved in and accepted his point of view. Often people just used to disappear. I remember one man who was a regular part of our after-work party in the pub telling stories about Maxwell. His office was in the same building as ours and one day we called to collect him. The office had been closed down and was now emptied of furniture. We assumed he'd been fired, but no-one ever said anything about him and we've never seen him from that day to this.

'Of course, Maxwell used to ritually humiliate people. He'd call them in on a particular day every week to give him a report and then humiliate them in front of their bosses, colleagues and subordinates. There were ritual sackings as well. He liked to have an audience. He would often ask for quite detailed reports about various parts of the business and then he would ignore them. He did this to me once: I gave him a report and he never even looked at it. He also used to throw them out of the office windows without reading them – you could sometimes see the loose papers fluttering down.

'Needless to say he lied. I remember going to him after taking an in-depth look at BPC's publishing companies and finding that not one of them was making a profit. He said that was rubbish and refused to accept it. The next day there was a report in the *Financial Times* quoting Maxwell as saying that the publishing companies had now got over their problems and he was happy to say all were currently trading profitably.'

*　　*　　*

Maxwell's secrecy was legendary. In the British Ministry of Defence and other sensitive organizations information is given on what is described as 'a need-to-know basis'. Inside Maxwell's organization his former right-hand man Peter Jay is said to have quipped 'if you need to know, you aren't told.'

Nick Grant claims that those working for Maxwell often had to gossip with other staff to find out what their boss was up to. On one occasion Grant spoke to a union negotiator during a labour dispute. The negotiator told him what the score was. He then went to a meeting with Maxwell and made the mistake of quoting the man's views. Grant says: 'This guy was fired. I felt extremely difficult about it. I am glad to say he was later reinstated, but, as you can imagine, he was less than pleased with me. I hadn't intended to drop him in it. I'd only just joined the Mirror Group and made the mistake of thinking we were all on the same side.'

* * *

'Bob Maxwell purported to be the white knight during a hostile bid for the printing company McCorquodale. I was asked to be the Chairman if a management buyout took place,' remembers Michael Stoddart of Electra Trust. As a result Maxwell bombarded him with phone calls and faxes.

'I was at home one Sunday afternoon in rural Shropshire when the phone went. It was Robert Maxwell. We talked for a short time and he said he wanted to send me further details by fax. I explained that I didn't have a fax at home.

'He said: "Never mind, get your man to clear the paddock and I will send the helicopter." I didn't have a man, but we did have a paddock. Half an hour later the helicopter landed and a man came bounding over to me with the papers. He waited until I had read them and then took off.'

* * *

Maxwell's corporate films were produced for him by Paul Ellis of Crown Communications. Sometimes Maxwell's sons, Kevin and Ian, would suggest changes but ask Ellis not to tell the old man. Maxwell regarded himself as a film-maker, which made life difficult for Ellis. 'The first film we made for him was to cost £96,000 and we had agreed payment in three equal stages. I went to see Mr Maxwell to give a progress report. After the meeting he said: "I suppose you will want paying now?"

'"That would be nice," I said.

'So Maxwell just pulled out a cheque book and wrote out

a cheque for £32,000. That was the first time I had seen the boss of a large company pick up a cheque book and sign such a large sum off, on the spot, without it having to go through the accounts department and layers of bureaucracy. Mind you, it was the only time he did it. I suppose he wanted to show me who was the boss of the company and just how much power he had.

'He was always trying to alter the film scripts. I remember a meeting at his offices in Holborn. In one small room he had an ornate desk with a seat behind and a window behind that. There was a magnificent view of the London skyline. Also in the room were three or four easy chairs with a low table in between. I had finished the film script and he called me in to discuss it. He had one of his aides with him and during the course of the discussion he lost his temper. He called me every four letter word he could. He criticized the script, insisted on rewriting it and kept thumping the table, telling me I was totally incompetent.

'In the middle of this huge row there was suddenly a knock at the door and his butler, Joseph, walked in with a large cake covered in candles. I wondered what was going on and was told that it was the birthday of one of his secretaries. She came in and there followed a little celebration. We all drank coffee and everyone was jolly. As soon as that was over and Joseph, the secretary and other staff had left, he began the row all over again – at exactly the place we had left off before the butler walked in.'

*   *   *

'The first time I met Robert Maxwell he was wearing a black suit, a black cape with red satin lining and a red satin bow tie. He looked grotesque since he weighed all of 360lb,' recalls Jan Constantine, litigation counsel for Macmillan in the United States from 1988 to 1991.

'We were always in the courts for Mr Maxwell, particularly when he was being sued for not going ahead with an acquisition. I remember one occasion when he was being taken to court and sued for 10 million dollars. This was all to do with a company in Chicago. We had to take statements from Mr Maxwell and counsel for both sides had to come over from the United States to London in order to take depositions. But at the last minute we got a call telling us that Mr Maxwell was unwell and that he could not travel the few blocks to the plaintiff's counsel's office. He insisted that we should arrange to come over to Maxwell House and take his statement there.

'We had to go before a judge in Wisconsin to ask him for permission to take the statements in this way. He said he would grant permission but only if he could be assured that Mr Maxwell was ill and only if Mr Maxwell were confined to his home. We told him this was the case and were granted permission to take his testimony at his office and home in London.

'The deposition took place on a Saturday, the day of the Grand National. Mr Maxwell was in a dressing gown, and at about 2pm his daughter Ghislaine knocked on the door. We had finished our business and Mr Maxwell thanked us, said goodbye and excused himself, saying he was going upstairs to lie down. We gathered from Ghislaine that she intended to go to watch the Grand National at Aintree near Liverpool.

'As we gathered our papers up and were walking out of the building we heard the helicopter start up. I wondered if it were taking Mr Maxwell anywhere. I had this awful feeling that it was flying him to Aintree. I just hoped that he wasn't photographed there or we might all end up in court back in the States for contempt. After all, the judge had stipulated that Mr Maxwell should be confined to his home, otherwise he would have had to go to the plaintiff's lawyer's office to swear the depositions.

'I never saw any photographs of Maxwell at the horserace and never heard any more about it. But I have always wondered.'

Susan Heilbron was general counsel for Maxwell from

April until November 1990. She was effectively the number one in his legal department in the United States. She left after what she described as 'a professional disagreement over some documents I wouldn't sign'. Susan Heilbron had joined Maxwell after working for Donald Trump.

'Maxwell very much wanted to have Donald Trump's lawyer. This was before there was any hint of Donald's business empire getting into trouble; but very soon after I joined Robert Maxwell the cracks in Donald's business began to appear. Maxwell wasn't pleased. He had hired a "trophy lawyer" and I am sure he thought his trophy was now tarnished. He used to boast about having Donald Trump's lawyer but that quickly stopped.

'After working for him for a short time there was a meeting at Berlitz; I think it was their AGM. Anyway, I decided to go there because it was part of the Maxwell publishing empire. The meeting took place in a hotel and I walked into a room which had a desk with Maxwell and his appointees behind it. When I arrived Maxwell got up, walked around the desk and strolled towards me. Before he reached me he started screaming "How can you do this to me? How can you have let this happen?" I asked him what his problem was and he pointed towards the dais and said "Look over there!"

'All I could see were the other members of the board and a nameplate for each of them, For example, opposite the centre chair the name tag said: Robert Maxwell, Chairman. On the next to it was Kevin Maxwell whose name tag read simply Kevin Maxwell, Chief Executive Officer. Robert Maxwell was screaming and yelling because the tags had the names written on only one side. He said he wanted them written on the other side too so that everyone on the table could see who they were sitting next to.

'Now, I could understand that if the people on the platform were not familiar with each other; but in this case some of his fellow directors were actually members of his own family, and those that weren't he had appointed himself.

'At first I thought he was joking but I quickly realized that he was not. So I asked a junior member of staff to write down the names using a felt tip pen on the other side of the tags.

'Later I found out that he had called everybody that had ever said anything nice about me and asked them how they could have recommended me. Donald Trump called me later. He and all the others Maxwell phoned thought Maxwell was crazy. I am convinced it was all because he felt he could no longer name-drop about me. He only hired me so that he could tell people he had bought Donald Trump's lawyer, and when he no longer felt able to do that I was of no value to him.'

*   *   *

Robert Maxwell hated to lose. This was a trueism in all the departments of his life. Jan Constantine remembers that sometimes this obsession cost him money.

'Again we were in court defending an action brought by the owners of a company which Maxwell had said he would take over but in the end had not. In the contracts which are drawn up in these circumstances there are certain clauses which have to be fulfilled before the takeover goes ahead. If they are not carried out it often allows the interested party to pull out at the last minute. In any event the plaintiffs had made an offer through the court to settle for four cents on the dollar. This would have meant that Maxwell would have had to pay $1.1 million plus about half a million dollars in legal fees. When this proposition was put to Maxwell, he said: "I would rather spend $100 to defend my position when I know I am in the right, than $10 to capitulate."

'We had been asked to make special arrangements for Maxwell's arrival to appear before the court. We were in a town in the Mid West and the finest suite had been booked at the best hotel; I remember it had a jacuzzi and a piano. We had been told that Mr Maxwell wanted the suite fully staffed and that he had to have hot tea and hot food available

24 hours a day. The tea was made in a silver tea pot and was changed every hour.

'I arrived at about 9 o'clock at night. Maxwell was due to arrive at 4 o'clock the following morning at the local airport. I went out to greet him with a number of other staff and a couple of limousines. Four o'clock came and went and there was no sign of Maxwell, so I phoned the airport in New York to see if Maxwell's plane had left there. I was told it had never arrived. Then I phoned the airport in Britain and again I was told the plane hadn't yet taken off. The trial was due to start in about five hours so there was no way Mr Maxwell was going to make that.

'I phoned his office to find out what might have happened. I was asked if I would like to speak to Mr Maxwell; I said that I would. He told me that due to "unforeseen technical difficulties" he was unable to leave London. He told me to apologize to the judge and say he was sorry he couldn't be there! He never apologized to the people who'd waited hours for him at the airport, nor did he ever say why neither he nor any of his staff in London didn't have the courtesy to telephone and tell us he wasn't coming.

'I was angry and didn't think that his non-appearance would do our case any good. But in the end I thought "What the hell, it's not my money!" And so I went back to the hotel suite, ate Mr Maxwell's breakfast and prepared other witnesses for the trial in luxury.

'When I appeared in court at 9am I apologized to the judge, explaining the non-appearance of Maxwell as best I could. He eventually ruled against MCC and the case was settled after I left the company.

'Sure enough, the upshot of the case was that Maxwell had to pay out about $2.5 million dollars plus $500,000 legal fees. If he'd settled at the outset it would only have cost about $1.5 million. But as I remember it, the bill had to be paid by Maxwell Communication Corporation anyway.'

*   *   *

Bob Cole, Maxwell's hardpressed Press Officer, was at the centre of the events of November and December 1991. It was he who had to stand on the steps of the company headquarters and announce to the world that Robert Maxwell was dead. Over the succeeding weeks – as the details of Maxwell's plundering of pension funds came out – Bob Cole found himself having to put across the company line while at the same time grappling with his own emotions about what had happened. Cole had worked for Maxwell for three decades and he, too, is now without a pension. Maxwell Communication is in administration and although he's been working with the authorities to try and help them unravel what happened, the chances of his keeping his job are slim. In his mid-fifties, Cole knows that in the midst of a recession there aren't many jobs going for the likes of him. He says he often wishes Maxwell would return so that he could ask him just one question: 'Why?' Despite Cole's bitter disappointment he still has many fond memories of his former employer.

'I remember going to Robert Maxwell one day and asking for him to authorize what was in the company terms a small payment. He studied it carefully and I said that to him, surely, it was petty cash? He replied: "Petty cash? Petty cash? No cash is petty when it belongs to me."

'One of his favourite sayings was Murphy's Law ("Anything that can go wrong, will go wrong"). He used to say that Maxwell's rider to Murphy's law was that "Murphy was a f.....g optimist."'

*   *   *

Over the years Maxwell had many tussles with the satirical magazine *Private Eye*. In 1985 he won a famous libel case against them. During the course of the hearing, Maxwell broke down in the witness box and told the court that his whole family had been wiped out by the Nazis. After winning £5,000 damages and £50,000 further punitive damages, Maxwell returned to the Mirror building in triumph.

A few days later he gathered together a team of journalists and told them he was going to publish a book about the libel case. Toby Roxburgh worked for Macdonald Futura and was to be the publishing expert on the project. He says Maxwell drove everyone crazy with his constant interference.

'There were half a dozen people from the *Mirror* involved in the project. Joe Haines and three other journalists did the writing and I was the editor. There was a lawyer there, too, to make sure that Maxwell didn't go over the top, because he was constantly trying to rewrite what had been written. He wanted to choose the photographs and it was laughable to see the great man – all 22 stone of him – on his hands and knees handing me photographs and saying: "What about this one, or what about that?" We were all under tremendous pressure to finish the book in the time. At a crucial stage I remember him asking me to make yet more changes and I blew my top.

'I said to him: "If you want your book published you can f.....g do it yourself! I have a motorcycle dispatch rider waiting for it and any more messing about and it will never be printed."

'He shut up. I think I am the only person ever to have spoken to him like that and got away with it.'

*   *   *

In 1947 the managing director of the specialist legal publishers Butterworth's was John Whitlock, who was a close family friend of Bob Cole's. Back in those immediate post-war years Robert Maxwell was yet to make his way in the world. Cole recalls that, some years after Whitlock and Maxwell met, Whitlock told him how the two men had ended up doing business together.

'Butterworth's were having a board meeting. John Whitlock was in the Chair and other board members included Quintin Hogg, later Lord Hailsham, and Recorder Denning, later Lord Denning, Master of the Rolls. John's secretary interrupted proceedings to inform him that there was a young man outside who wanted to see him. Whitlock told his secretary that he couldn't see anyone at the moment and to tell the young man that he couldn't possibly interrupt an important board meeting just to see him. A few minutes later the secretary was back again, saying that the young man was very insistent. Again John said he couldn't see him at the moment.

'The secretary passed on the message but came back a few moments later saying the young man had said that Sir Charles Hambro had recommended that he see Mr Whitlock. Sir Charles was the Chairman of Hambro's bank but, more importantly, he and John Whitlock had both fought in the First World War. John told his secretary he would see the young man but not at the moment. He said that he should make an appointment and come back and that is exactly what he did. Of course, the young man was Robert Maxwell.

'When Maxwell returned he outlined to John a number of projects – all to do with publishing material of a scientific nature. In view of Butterworth's lack of expertise in this area a joint venture company was set up with the German publishers Springer. It was called Springer-Butterworth and that is how Robert Maxwell got started. Some years later Maxwell bought out the company but was told that he couldn't keep their name. It was changed to Pergamon Press.

'The story doesn't end there because, some years after that, Maxwell decided he wanted to bid for Butterworth's. Maxwell used to say of John Whitlock: "Yes, he is a great man and the head of a great publishing house. Of course, I taught him all he knows about publishing."

'Anyway, the thought of Maxwell as a hostile bidder for the company he'd built up really upset John and he went around the world looking for a "white knight" to save the company from Maxwell's clutches. Eventually he found one in the shape of IPC, the company that eventually became Reed International, and that is why they own Butterworth's today. John was upset that Maxwell wanted to take over his company after he had given Maxwell a start in the business.

It wasn't the way things were done in this country in those days. Maxwell seemed unable to grasp the concept of never biting the hand that feeds you.'

But then, Maxwell knew no rules but his own. He let nothing and no one stand in his way, as Sir Bernard Audley knows only too well.

'He worked Saturdays, Sundays and all through the week. One Saturday morning he decided he was going to move his office over the road, above *The European*. The Assistant Editor was away and his office was locked. But Maxwell wanted to get in, so he sent for his security staff. They went over to the office and Maxwell, armed with a crowbar, broke the door down. So we have this extraordinary person who could entertain these visions of grandeur but at the same time was thinking like a peasant.'

*   *   *

In March 1991 Robert Maxwell unexpectedly announced that he was to step down as Chairman of Maxwell Communication Corporation. He said he would hand over to a 'senior City figure' and that his two sons, Ian and Kevin, would work to the new Chairman.

The idea, or so it was mooted, was that this would enable Maxwell to concentrate on the newspapers – the *Mirror* flotation and saving the New York *Daily News*. A few days later Sir Michael Richardson, of Maxwell's brokers Smith New Court, told Maxwell that Peter Walker, former Conservative cabinet minister and a fellow director in the broking house, had agreed to become Chairman of MCC.

Richardson then said to Maxwell: 'Bob, there is a slight problem though, Peter finds it difficult to accept the position while his own firm is still owed fees. As you know there have been repeated reminders. Could we remove that problem?'

Maxwell picked up a phone straight away and bellowed at someone at the other end: 'Why do we still owe Smith New Court their fees? I've told you so often to pay.'

Richardson smiled at the performance. Less than four

months later Peter Walker announced that he would not after all be taking over from Maxwell as Chairman of Maxwell Communication Corporation. He said MCC was a 'terrific company' but that he thought that it had become an American company and as such should be run from there. He recommended it should be demerged and run from New York but added that he did not want to leave Britain and had therefore decided not to become Chairman of MCC. Though it was true that something like 80 per cent of MCC's profits came from the US, analysts in the City believed there was a hidden agenda. It was really from this point that Maxwell's media empire would slide inexorably into the abyss.

*   *   *

After Maxwell's death and the revelations about the money that had been plundered from pension funds, administrators decided to sell the contents of Maxwell's penthouse apartment on top of Maxwell House, behind the Mirror Group building at Holborn Circus in London.

The auction was to be held by Sotheby's. There was the usual press preview, to which I was invited. What I found remarkable about the apartment was that it told me nothing about the man who lived there. We were told that Maxwell had employed an interior designer, but nevertheless I felt there should be at least some vestige of the publisher himself. I suppose in a sense the huge television screen in the sitting room was one of the few personal items. Something else which struck me was that in the media magnate's study the desk faced into the room. Behind him Maxwell had a wonderful view over the city: you could see St Paul's Cathedral, and I remember thinking it was a strong man who would have had his desk facing away from such a view!

At the auction, held in February 1992, the contents of the apartment raised £478,000. Although some of the quality pieces were bought cheaply there were some surprising results for novelty items. Robert Maxwell would certainly have been upset to hear that his 'Governors' baseball caps sold to his arch-rivals, the *Sun* newspaper for £1,100 each. They were to be given away as prizes.

The man who organized the sale was Leslie Weller, Sothebys' Director of European Furniture. 'It was a strange mixture of styles, with some nice European paintings and a very fine Georgian dining table with some modern chairs which didn't actually seem out of place. But it was obvious that Mr Maxwell didn't really have any interest in buying items for the apartment. He had hired an interior designer, given him a budget and told him to furnish the place. He may or may not have given them some idea of what he liked or didn't like, but I suppose he had other things to do.

'It was a striking apartment, octagonal in shape, with the magnificent views from most rooms across the City of London and St Paul's Cathedral clearly visible.

'There was one thing that struck me, though. When we came in to catalogue the contents, there was a copy of Robert Maxwell's biography *Maxwell* by Joe Haines in every one of the main rooms, including the bedrooms.'

Politics

Robert Maxwell's brief but turbulent parliamentary career began with the Labour Party's victory in 1964, when he won the Buckingham constituency for Labour for the first time since 1951. But it soon became apparent that he was not enough of a diplomat to succeed in Parliament.

Maxwell's mentor, Richard Crossman, told him he could not expect an immediate Government post and advised him to 'lie low for six months'. But Maxwell became the first MP ever to deliver his maiden speech on the very first day of the new Parliament. He boasted about 'having got in first' without realizing that he'd angered his own front bench by taking three times as long over his speech as he should have done. During the next few days he constantly interrupted Opposition speakers to score points: the new member wanted to shine. Maxwell seemed to believe that only he could change the country and if people would listen to him all the nation's problems would be solved.

Any ministerial ambitions Maxwell might have had disappeared when, a few weeks later, he attacked Parliamentary traditions and accused his own party of conspiring with the Opposition to approve the annual cost of Britain's embassies without a debate. He was dubbed 'the biggest gasbag in the Commons' by the Crossbencher column in the *Daily Express*.

At the end of his first year in the House, Maxwell took the unusual step of presenting his local party with 'an invoice' of his work. He told them he had spent 3,260 hours working on constituency business, including 1,580 inside Westminster. He had made 92 contributions or interventions in debates and asked 65 questions; he had written 4,000 letters on behalf of constituents, including 215 to ministers, and he had led 20 deputations to them. He had met 780 constituents on personal matters; he had attended 115 public meetings, made 6,000 telephone calls and travelled 15,000 miles.

In March 1966, Prime Minister Harold Wilson called a general election to try to improve his Government's slender majority of four. Maxwell did his bit and was returned with an increased majority of 2,254. Though it was a personal triumph for Maxwell, it was immediately apparent that he wouldn't be invited to join the Government and would be unlikely to be asked to in the lifetime of that Parliament.

Maxwell's frustration was obvious. In order to harness some of his business know-how and energy, Richard Crossman invited him to become Chairman of the House of Commons Catering Committee. It was suggested that if Maxwell made a success of the committee it might persuade Harold Wilson that he could run a government department. But it seems clear now that no member of the cabinet wanted Maxwell as a junior minister.

Maxwell threw himself into the catering job. He claimed to have wiped out a deficit of £53,000 in one year by negotiating a grant from the Treasury, reducing the number of staff, bringing down the quality of meals and selling the entire stock of vintage wine. His success, contrary to his expections, made him even less popular. Question-time in the Commons was tailor made for any MP who fancied a cheap jibe at the socialist millionaire. Maxwell was asked about the substitution of powdered milk for fresh, the introduction of processed chips instead of potatoes, and the substitution of sugary biscuits for decent plain ones in the tea bar. After two years as Commons culinary supremo, Maxwell retired from the committee.

Britain was hit by a wave of strikes as Wilson appealed

for the 'Dunkirk spirit' to halt the country's economic decline. In the House of Commons Maxwell launched the 'Think British – Buy British' Campaign. He attracted tremendous publicity, but the good work fell apart when Maxwell used a number of celebrities in an advertising campaign without telling them. He also failed to grasp the inconsistency of his telling people to buy British while he insisted on printing Pergamon's books and journals in eastern Europe because it was cheaper.

By 1969 Maxwell's parliamentary career had still failed to take wing. He had become disillusioned with Labour's policies – and some of those in his local constituency party had become disillusioned with him, feeling that if you weren't 100 per cent for Maxwell he assumed you were against him. Maxwell made the mistake of telling the public that if his bid for the *News of the World* was successful he would resign his seat. In the end it didn't matter. The election was called for 18 June 1970 and Maxwell lost by 2,521 votes to the Conservative William Benyon. It was effectively the end of Maxwell's political career. He tried to secure adoption during the 1974 campaign, and even wanted to stand as a Euro MP; but in the end Maxwell finally had to admit to himself that he wasn't going to be Prime Minister, and he turned his attention firmly to the business world.

*   *   *

The Labour MP Tam Dalyell was elected to Parliament two years before Maxwell. They became friends and Dalyell formed a bond with Maxwell's family over the next 27 years, though he was never involved in Maxwell's businesses. He recalls: 'It was the autumn of 1964. The House of Commons was packed for the first major foreign affairs debate of the incoming Labour Government. On the Opposition front bench were Alec Home who had been Prime Minister, Rab Butler, who had been there for more than 35 years, Iain Macleod, Reggie Maudling and Ted Heath. Up gets a figure after the Speaker has said: "Order, Order."

'"On a point of order," says the upstanding MP, "I am Captain Robert Maxwell, MC."

'The House was transfixed: nobody ever announced themselves in such a way. Bob Maxwell spoke for 17 minutes on a point of order. It was ostensibly a complaint about the shortcomings of the commercial section of the British embassy in Washington. But – surprise, surprise – the speech was really about the annoyances suffered at the hands of these officials by Bob Maxwell's own businesses.'

The reaction to Maxwell's outburst was predictable on both sides of the political divide, according to Tam Dalyell: amusement on the Tory benches and horror amongst the Labour supporters. 'Harold Wilson was fiddling with his spectacles nervously. George Brown was muttering all sorts of imprecations under his breath. Ray Gunter was saying for all to hear that Maxwell was a traitor to the working class. Crossman was saying, "Bob, what the hell do you think you are doing?" And Jim Callaghan was looking as he always does in embarrassing situations. On the Opposition front bench Rab Butler was unable to suppress a smile and this extraordinary figure just went on and on. Eventually Maxwell sat down.

'Later that evening, as Secretary of the Labour Party standing conference on the sciences, I telephoned Harold Thompson, Professor of Chemistry at Oxford (and later Chairman of the Football Association). After we had done our business I said: "What do you think about the behaviour of our mutual friend, Bob Maxwell?"

'Quick as a flash Thompson replied: "Tam, you just be thankful that Bob Maxwell waited until the Queen sat down."'

Tam Dalyell knew Bob and Betty Maxwell for years and was horrified by the revelations after his death. He told me that Mrs Maxwell said that the man she married and the man she knew over the last 18 months of his life were not the same person.

Dalyell recalls that Maxwell rang him from New York 11

days before his death. The MP told Maxwell that his friends should be told if he were a Mossad agent. 'He was very emotional about it, but said that he wasn't.'

* * *

Gyles Brandreth, writer, celebrity and now Conservative MP for Chester, was at Oxford with two of Maxwell's children, Anne and Phillip. He remembers lavish parties given for the students at the family home, Headington Hill Hall. There was a 'tented village of delights'. Mr Maxwell's hospitality couldn't have been more generous.

There used to be a party every summer at the Hall, where Maxwell would entertain a 'thousand or so' of his closest friends to celebrate his birthday.

'I recall being invited to one of these because I was involved in writing a book which was being published by one of Mr Maxwell's firms. I remember wandering around and being vaguely aware that it didn't seem to matter which room I was in, I always seemed to be able to hear the great man. I became curious so I decided to do a bit of detective work. I found that in every room there was a speaker and on closer inspection of Mr Maxwell himself I realized that he was wearing a small clip-on microphone on his lapel which he was using to amplify his voice and send it out somehow through the speakers. I also noticed that he could turn the volume down when he wanted to have a private conversation with someone.'

* * *

Supporters and opponents alike agreed that Robert Maxwell was a good constituency MP. Indeed, he is still remembered fondly by many in Buckingham as the MP who, if a voter had a problem, would go straight out and fix it. He was looked up to by many in the way a local squire would be – and he often behaved like one. The party faithful would be bussed to a Christmas gathering at his home in Oxford every year. He paid the membership subs of many Labour Party

members and even held the parliamentary selection meetings
on his own premises.

Kate Moulin is a former Buckingham Labour Party
member, who now works for Edinburgh city council: 'I'm
trying to place it in time. I think it was June 1973. I had
just moved to Olney. I was going through the town centre
pushing my young baby in a pram, when I saw Robert
Maxwell canvassing for the Labour Party. He stopped me
and asked if I was a member of the party. I told him I had
just moved to the area. He suggested I join and we got
chatting. I told him I'd been a management consultant before
I had the baby, and he offered me a job on the spot. He
told me to go along to the local factory, Bumper, Haldane
and Maxwell, and ask to speak to the manager. He said I
would be expected.

'The next day I did just that. When I approached the local
manager he raised his eyes to the heavens as if to say: "Oh
no, not another one!" Then he told me the only job he could
offer me would be packing books. I got the impression that
Mr Maxwell offered many local people jobs and that some
of them actually ended up working for him.'

Ray Thomas was also a Labour Party member in Buckingham. He isn't alone in recalling the publisher's personality:
'What I remember most vividly about him was the amazing
presence of the man. At selection committees he would defeat
anyone. He once defeated the former Government minister,
Ivor Richards, and the future MPs Stuart Holland and Geoff
Edge, as well as a BBC Television correspondent.'

Another local party member was Geoff Peters. Like many
of those Robert Maxwell disliked, he worked for the Open
University at nearby Milton Keynes. He moved into the area
in 1970–71, he says, just after Maxwell had lost his seat. In
the 1974 campaign he vividly remembers the local Labour
Party poster: 'It didn't have any words on it, certainly no
mention of the Labour Party. The whole poster was taken
up by a full-colour picture of Robert Maxwell himself. I
wish I had kept one.

'I heard a story about a neighbouring Labour constituency party that found itself in financial trouble. Maxwell offered to bale them out – provided they handed over the freehold of their Labour hall. He said the hall was on a 20-year lease anyway and at the end of it he would renew it on just as favourable terms. Of course, when the time came he told them to get out.'

Ray Phillips worked closely with Maxwell in those early years. He is a former mayor and lives in Winslow, south-east of Buckingham.

'He used his MP's salary to buy food for every old age pensioner in the constituency at Christmas. He also used to take groups of workers up to the House of Commons. He used to hold lunches at his home, Headington Hill Hall, for party workers. I went to many of them.

'He loved mixing with ordinary people. The first time I met him he was coming to my house before going to a local pub for a lunchtime drink. He turned up in the Rolls Royce and I said: "I'm not travelling in that. We can take my car." He never argued, just got into my car and off we went. He was very fond of chatting to the locals and having a pint. He would sort out people's problems, however small. I remember him once concerning himself about guttering coming off a council house. He would go to any lengths to help.

'When the Labour Party won the 1945 election two bro-thers, Bill and Phil Neal, who ran the Bell public house in Winslow, said they would bar the front door and would not open it until Labour had been ousted. The pub had been a family concern for 120 years, and both men were staunch Tories. Little did they know that their move would receive so much publicity. When Maxwell won his seat in 1964 and again in 1966 the pub's customers all used a side door. Needless to say Maxwell, as the local Labour MP, was not exactly welcome. In the end – and to win a bet – Maxwell managed to get inside the pub, where he spent some time with the brothers discussing the world.'

Geoff Peters recalls how Maxwell often used to enlist the help of his local business managers in some of the Buckingham campaigns.

'I remember canvassing on behalf of the Labour Party in Olney. The campaign was organized by Robert Maxwell, though he and Betty didn't go out themselves. Mr Maxwell had invited us for tea at the home of the managing director of a small publishing concern he owned. This was in the days when Labour canvassers didn't have to wear suits, and wellingtons would do as footwear. After we had finished canvassing Betty Maxwell picked us up in her Jaguar and took us to tea. You could see the MD didn't really want us there, but nevertheless he had laid out his best china. He looked like a real Tory voter, but he was obliged to impress the boss and his wife.'

Geoff Edge moved into Maxwell's marginal constituency in 1970; he was another lecturer to join the Open University, but later became an MP himself. He quickly fell out with Captain Bob over Edge's plan to set up a branch of the Labour Party in an area in which Maxwell owned a house. Apparently doing this without asking the permission of the great parliamentarian was tantamount to treason. The animosity between Edge and Maxwell grew, so that when Edge stood for election as secretary of Bletchley Labour Party there was a rival, Maxwell-supported candidate.

'The meeting was crowded, and when I was declared the winner, women had to be carried out of the hall sobbing, such was the degree of influence Maxwell had.' Maxwell tried to have Geoff Edge thrown out of the Labour Party at the time when Edge was about to win the nomination to stand as parliamentary candidate for the midlands seat of Aldridge and Brownhills, which he eventually won. Edge was advised by the Labour peer Lord Underhill to go into hiding for a week until he was selected: Lord Underhill said that if no one knew where he was, he couldn't be expelled from the party!

Through all his dealings with Maxwell, Edge remembers

one of his characteristics above all others. 'He had a great gift for languages and an ability never to forget a face or a name.' He recalls Maxwell saying that someone would 'send the bums in', if they didn't pay up. He thought at the time that the sophisticated use of the old term for bailiff was remarkable for a man whose first language wasn't English.

*   *   *

Throughout his life Maxwell told anyone who would listen that he was the confidant of many of the world's leaders. He was particularly fond of being photographed with the top men in the Communist world and eventually gave the impression that he was a friend of the Soviet leader Mikhail Gorbachev. Paul Ellis, who worked for Maxwell for four years, had always wondered how Maxwell did it. Suddenly he had an idea. He confronted Maxwell and told him that he now knew how it was that Maxwell was so often seen in the company of these world statesmen. Ellis had discovered that Maxwell's meetings with them often coincided with the publication by Pergamon of collections of their speeches. He concluded that Maxwell rang the leaders up to tell them that their book of speeches was about to be published, adding that – coincidentally – he would shortly be in Moscow, Berlin, Bucharest or wherever, and would like to present a specially bound volume to them and a number of other copies of the book for their friends. Maxwell would then fly off and have his photograph taken with whichever leader it happened to be. In the case of Gorbachev one such meeting was reported in the Soviet newspaper *Pravda*, where the account of his visit made no mention of the books but said the two men had talked for nearly two and a half hours.

When Ellis put his theory to the publisher, all Maxwell would say was: 'That's right.' If he was telling the truth, the method certainly proved a cheap, simple and effective means of obtaining and maintaining his image as a power broker for world leaders. It no doubt enhanced his credit rating as well.

Maxwell went to great lengths to be seen as a key player in world events. Mike Kirkham, former head of television research for AGB, recalls an encounter he experienced one weekend.

'The phone rang at home on Friday evening and my 10-year-old daughter answered it.

'She said: "It's Mr Maxwell to speak to you."

'I could picture him in his office, sitting at his desk with millions of telephones on it.

'"Are you sitting down?" he said. "I have some good news for you. I mean, would I phone you on a Friday evening if it weren't good news?"

'I thought: "Yes, you would, you old so and so."

'"Come and see me tomorrow morning," he said, "and bring Stephen Buck with you. It must be before 10 o'clock because I'm going to see Gorbachev."

'When we went to see Maxwell he announced some scheme and Stephen told him we should get ready with the publicity campaign for it. Maxwell told him sternly: "We do not need publicity. What we want is good solid achievement. I am a man that shuns publicity."

'With that we left. On Monday morning I was at home having a shave and listening to the *Today* programme on Radio 4. The news carried a report about Gorbachev's visit to the United States. Apparently he had left Washington for San Francisco and stopped over in Minneapolis for lunch with local businessmen. The report said that he was met there by British media tycoon Robert Maxwell in what was described as a surprise visit. Mr Maxwell had announced the formation of the Gorbachev-Maxwell Institute of Sciences, to which he had donated $100 million.

'I thought: "And this is the man who shuns publicity."'

Susan Heilbron, Maxwell's lawyer in the United States for a few months in 1990, adds some significant details to this episode:

'When Maxwell met Gorbachev in Minneapolis and announced the setting up of the Gorbachev-Maxwell Institute, he said he would give $50 million to the institute provided that another 50 million were donated by the businessmen of Minneapolis. This part of the deal wasn't as well publicized as the rest of it, but basically it meant that, if the local community didn't raise their half, Maxwell didn't have to give a dime. That is exactly what happened, and he never paid a penny. He did this sort of thing quite often, saying he was contributing some vast sum to the setting up of an organization, milk his announcement for all the publicity it was worth, and then just forget about it. He promised the Brooklyn Polytechnic Institute $10 million, but they never received a penny either.'

*　　*　　*

During one of Maxwell's meetings with Gorbachev, photographs were taken of the two great men shaking hands. In front of them was a table with a jug of water and glasses on it. When the photos were developed the handshake was actually obscured by the glassware on the table. Maxwell is reported to have spent several thousand pounds having the photos touched up so that the handshake would be clearly visible.

*　　*　　*

'Of course,' remembers Sir Bernard Audley, 'Maxwell prided himself on his political contacts around the world. He really regarded himself as an international statesman and power broker. In 1987 he was the guest of the Jewish Blind Society's annual businessman's lunch. He told his fellow guests that amongst those who had asked his advice in the past was the late Soviet leader Leonid Brezhnev. Maxwell said Brezhnev always asked him for a foreign policy analysis whenever the publisher was passing through Moscow.

"'I recall one occasion," said Maxwell, "when, after the consumption of a lot of vodka, he asked me what I thought might have happened if Nikita Khruschev had been assassinated instead of John Kennedy.

"'I replied that I could only predict for certain that Mr Onassis would certainly not have married Mrs Khruschev.'"

If Maxwell liked a story he would keep on using it. He certainly liked the Onassis-Khruschev tale – but he told it for the very last time at a dinner in New York. It did not go down at all well. Maxwell had neglected to notice that his fellow guests included Bobby Kennedy's widow, Ethel, who was sitting at his own table, and one of Bobby Kennedy's daughters.

*   *   *

As we have seen, Maxwell was always boasting about his influence in the Communist countries of Eastern Europe. No one is sure exactly what role he played in some of the hardline Stalinist countries. In Bulgaria there have been investigations into possible money-laundering by Maxwell, and these are still taking place. Ilka Eskanasi is a Bulgarian MP who orchestrated the official search into Maxwell's business and political links with Bulgaria.

'Maxwell's contacts in the former Communist regime were only at the highest level, and when he arrived he was treated like a foreign Prime Minister. He was visited by the President of Bulgaria and gave lengthy interviews on television and in the press. His opinion on anything seemed to be valued highly. In Bulgaria it was regarded as a privilege to meet Mr Maxwell. During his visits he showed a readiness to make many donations. He was said to have signed cheques for a million or two million pounds. But afterwards it emerged that, although he appeared on television saying he was going to do this or that and signing cheques for what appeared to be large sums of money, very little of this money actually found its way into the projects he claimed he was supporting. The problem we have is we do not know whether the money existed at all or whether the money did exist at one time and has either been squandered since his death or put into an account somewhere.'

*   *   *

Throughout his life Maxwell craved an audience. He wanted attention, but he wanted it in the way that a small child performing a song or reciting a poem wants attention: there must be nothing critical about it, just enthusiastic adulation. Now, in Maxwell's case nothing was straightforward, however simple it might have seemed. His fawning to the dictators of Eastern Europe, his publishing of biographies or speeches by them, were designed to enhance Maxwell's reputation as a global statesman. The remarkable thing is that he sustained this reputation for as long as he did.

In 1985 Robert Maxwell arrived in Warsaw on one of his many trips around and through the Iron Curtain. He was there to see the Polish head of state, General Jaruzelski. At that time Kevin Ruane was the BBC's Poland Correspondent. On Saturday, 25 May Ruane was delayed arriving for an official British Embassy function.

'I was late for a dinner given by the British Ambassador to Poland, John Morgan. His guest of honour was Robert Maxwell, who had just arrived in Warsaw to see General Jaruzelski and discuss the publication of the Polish leader's biography.

'I was late because, as BBC correspondent in Warsaw, I had spent most of the day in court. Jacek Kuron, one of the trade union Solidarity's leading advisers, was appealing against the verdict of a local misdemeanour court which had found him guilty of leading an anti-government demonstration on May Day and had sentenced him to three months in prison. Remarkably, the appeal court had accepted the evidence of defence witnesses that all that Kuron had done on the day in question was to negotiate a peaceful end to the affair when the marching demonstrators were halted and confronted by the police. Kuron was acquitted.

'This was quite surprising, for the authorities had only just launched a new, hard-line campaign against Solidarity. And only two days earlier three of Kuron's closest Solidarity colleagues – Adam Michnik, Bogdan Lis and Wladyslaw

Frasyniuk – had gone on trial in Gdansk, accused of foment-
ing unrest.

'By the time I reached the Ambassador's residence, the
host and his six other guests were already at the table. But
the Ambassador courteously assured me that he knew I was
going to be late and asked me what had happened.

'"Kuron has been acquitted," I said.

'"What?" said Wieslaw Gornicki, General Jaruzelski's
closest aide, a journalist who had assumed military rank
since the declaration of martial law and was a major, I think,
at the time. "Why was he acquitted?" he asked, in some
shock.

'"Possibly because he was innocent," said Roger Boyes of
The Times, the only other Western journalist present.

'Major Gornicki was not amused and retaliated by telling
me that he could give me interesting details about what
exactly Jacek Kuron was up to on the night martial law was
imposed. I was not particularly interested in any such details,
but it was Robert Maxwell who ended this interlude by
saying something that later found a wider audience when it
appeared in newsprint.

'"Of course, we admire your devotion and dedication,
Kevin," he said, "but really, you know, it's all over. Solidarity
is finished and my paper won't be writing about it again."

'This has stuck in my memory and I can still hear him
saying it. For the record, Jacek Kuron became a Minister –
and a very successful one – in the first Solidarity government
formed in the autumn of 1989.'

*   *   *

David Adler worked for Macmillan Inc. in the US. He
observed how Maxwell used to 'collect' politicians.

'Many of them worked for him. Senators John Tower,
Walter Mondale and Howard Baker were amongst those
whose company he actively sought. He once paid $200,000
to sit next to Ronald Reagan at a charity dinner in California.

'A few years before I began working for Mr Maxwell he

met and struck up a friendship with Senator Jesse Jackson. He was so friendly with him that he invited him to a Jewish function in New York. As you can imagine, this didn't go down too well, as the Jewish community hadn't really forgiven the senator for associating with known anti-semites in the run up to the Presidential election which George Bush won.'

* * *

During the British miners' strike in 1984, Maxwell organized a meeting at the Waldorf hotel in London between the Coal Board Chairman, Ian MacGregor, and the miners' leader, Arthur Scargill. Ray Buckton, the leader of the Railwaymen's union, ASLEF, was also trying to bring the two sides together and was at the meeting with Maxwell. At one point Buckton and Maxwell decided they had to go to ASLEF headquarters, which at the time was in Camden Town, with an important document.

As they were driving along Maxwell asked his chauffeur to let him know what was in his diary for the rest of the day. The chauffeur always kept a copy of the main diary in the car. He told Maxwell that he was due to meet a Professor X shortly. Suddenly Maxwell yelled: 'Stop the car! Stop the car!'

The car was stopped and Maxwell told his driver and Ray Buckton to get out and grab a taxi for the rest of the way to Camden Town. He said he had an urgent appointment. Maxwell then did a U-turn in the Rolls Royce and drove off in the opposite direction. A perplexed Buckton turned to the chauffeur and said: 'That's the first time that has happened to me. I have never been thrown out of a car before.'

* * *

Robert Maxwell seemed to regard himself as a head of state in temporary exile, and that an invitation from him should be treated as a royal command. When he was in America he often hosted parties aboard his yacht the *Lady Ghislaine*, either in New York or Washington. David Adler, public relations officer for publishers Macmillan Inc., remembers that Maxwell would decide to hold a party at short notice and then want embossed invitations printed and sent out within three days.

'Just before one of these parties I was having trouble getting an invitation to Senator Jesse Jackson. Robert Maxwell was due to fly in and I had to arrange for him and his staff to be met at the airport. I sent three limousines. When Mr Maxwell saw me later that day, he asked me why I hadn't met him personally. I explained that I was trying to arrange for Jesse Jackson and all these other important people to come to his party. He looked me in the eye and said: "David, I'm the only important person in your life."'

*   *   *

Two or three years ago Gyles Brandreth received a Christmas card from Robert Maxwell. 'I thought it was amusing, if not festive. At that seasonal time you expect to see a drawing of Christ on the front of a card. But this card had a photograph of Robert Maxwell taken at the fireworks display that always followed his birthday party, held every summer. Inside it simply read: "Merry Christmas."'

*   *   *

Maxwell boasted not only about his political influence on the world stage: he liked to think of himself as a big player at home in Britain. This image of himself was particularly strong in the autumn of Mrs Thatcher's last Government, as the editor of the *Daily Mirror*, Roy Greenslade, discovered when he received a more-than-routine call from his boss.

'"Clear the front page," Maxwell said. "I have a world exclusive." I tried to ensure my single-word reply covered all eventualities: "Really?"

'"Six cabinet ministers will resign in the morning. Only I know about it. We'll be ahead of the field. She's had it."

'At last, I thought, Maxwell was coming good. This was

a great story, Thatcher facing mutiny from within her own cabinet.

'Maxwell continued: "Not bad, eh? She'll have to go when they tell her."

"'How do we get into this?" I said, meaning that I needed a source, names of at least a couple of the six, possibly some kind of lead to pass on to Campbell and his political team.

'Maxwell exploded: "I've given you the f.....g scoop of the decade."

"'I realize that, Bob, but we can't just print it. We must have a source and we must have more facts." The phone was slammed down, so I rang Campbell in the Commons to give him the outline of Maxwell's tip. "Nonsense," he said. "Who says so?"

"'At the moment, only Maxwell."

'A newsdesk reporter put her head round my office door: "Maxwell's on the phone out here telling us he has a new splash."

'I rang Maxwell to explain that the first edition front page had already gone and meanwhile Campbell was checking out the story.

"'He can't check it," said Maxwell. "Who with?"

"'I think he is going to speak to Tim Renton [the Chief Whip]."

"'He won't know. This is much higher," said Maxwell. "You'll give the scoop away to everyone else. You don't know how to handle it."

'I kept as cool as I could. "Bob, I must attribute the story to someone. We cannot say six ministers will resign unless I have a source. We'll be a laughing stock. It will be bad for the *Mirror*."

"'Just print it," shouted Maxwell. "I am your Publisher. That should be good enough for you. Do you think I would tell you lies?"

'Minutes later he rang Campbell who had already effectively been told the story was untrue. Renton had informed him that Kenneth Clarke would probably resign if she

remained at No. 10, and that Chris Patten and Malcolm
Rifkind might possibly go, too. But there was no suggestion
that this would happen the next day, if at all. There was no
question of six ministers resigning.

'The barrage of calls – to me, to the newsdesk, to
Campbell – went on for more than an hour. Campbell arrived
in my office and we decided it was possible to write a
paragraph into our splash story saying that sources within the
cabinet were suggesting that some ministers might threaten to
resign unless Thatcher stood down. Maxwell was not placated
by this tiny amendment, which was tucked so far down the
splash it appeared on page three. In his final conversation
with me, past midnight, he said: "You have just thrown
away the scoop of the decade. You would have been the
news. You have made a bad error."

'Throughout the next day I made calls to Campbell to ask
if there were any hints of six ministers resigning. There were
not, and nobody did go in advance of Mrs Thatcher's own
resignation a day later.

'The intriguing question for me was how Maxwell had
come to be involved. Though aware of Maxwell's tenuous
hold on reality, I could not imagine him having made it all
up. Campbell got a glimpse the following Sunday when
Maxwell rang him to say: "I am very disappointed with you
for having missed the scoop of the decade. You showed bad
judgement and defective political antennae. It was the biggest
mistake of your career and I am considering your future. I
am not having the Political Editor of the *Daily Mirror* treat
me like some punter offering a story off the street. This was
high-grade information." Maxwell added darkly: "You have
sided with the Editor and ignored your Publisher."

'Campbell replied, not unreasonably, that as scoops go it
was hard to spot that he had missed one since six cabinet
ministers had not resigned. With his job on the line Campbell
asked if he could see Maxwell, who suggested he join him
in his apartment to watch the afternoon television interviews
of the three contestants for the leadership – Michael Hesel-

tine, Douglas Hurd and John Major. Once they were together Maxwell told Campbell it was bad enough that he had given him the scoop of the decade on a plate, "but for you not to see that you have missed it is even worse." Campbell said: "History proved me right. It came out exactly as I told you on Tuesday. The only resignation was hers. No other minister resigned."

"'They probably would have done," countered Maxwell, "if we had run the story!'"

*   *   *

Neil Kinnock, then leader of the Labour Party, invited Robert and Betty Maxwell for dinner. His guests were to meet at the Kinnocks' home in Ealing. At the appointed time, Robert Maxwell turned up in his chauffeur-driven Rolls Royce. At more or less the same time, Mrs Maxwell disembarks from her own chauffeur-driven Rolls Royce. Both the media tycoon and his wife were in formal dinner wear. The Kinnocks took them to eat at their favourite curry restaurant close to their home!

*   *   *

Maxwell the international statesman often got in the way of Maxwell the businessman. Board meetings could be difficult, even for seasoned campaigners like Sir Bernard Audley.

'I remember sitting in the board room at Maxwell House – it must have been about the first board meeting after AGB's takeover. There were the noble Lords Havers, Hoskyns, Morpeth and others, Geoffrey Robinson, Stoney, Napier, Buck, and I of course was in the Chair. Maxwell was my Deputy Chairman. Just as we had got the agenda under way, in comes Peter Jay.

'He says: "Bob, there's a telephone call for you."

"'Oh, do excuse me," says Maxwell, and left the room. A few minutes later Peter Jay came sauntering back into the meeting with him.

'Maxwell then said: "Now look, I don't want any more

calls. We have a board meeting going on here. No more calls." A short time later Peter Jay came in again. He apologized but said the President of Turkey was on the phone. Maxwell took the call in the boardroom. I heard him say: "Mr President, I have authority from Mikhail Gorbachev to take the heavy digging machinery into Armenia to help with the rescue operations following the earthquake. All I want from you is that you will keep your borders open for us. Thank you, Mr President, goodbye."

'He put the phone down and the meeting resumed.'

* * *

David Adler recalls, 'On one occasion I received a phone call from Mr Maxwell, telling me he was going to be in Washington in the next few days and could I arrange for him to call on President Bush. We tried to do it but in the end a meeting wasn't possible. I phoned back Mr Maxwell's London office but he wasn't there, so I left a message with a secretary that the meeting with the President wasn't on.

'Maxwell himself phoned back furious and said: "Never let a third secretary know of my arrangements regarding the President of the United States."'

* * *

As Bob Cole remembers, 'Maxwell loved going to the Labour Party conferences. He always threw a "Robert Maxwell Party". These were quite lavish affairs and were well attended. Maxwell made himself the centre of attention. On one particular occasion he was one of two key figures in a large group of people – the other was Neil Kinnock. The conversation was animated and Maxwell was taking an active part in it.

'All the time waiters were circulating with trays of drinks or baskets of fruit. One of these baskets caught Maxwell's eye as it went past him.

'Suddenly his great gorilla arm shot out and came back with the biggest Victoria plum I've ever seen. He split it in half and began to suck. The conversation was still in full swing and Maxwell was chomping on the plum. I watched with a horrified fascination. I could tell by watching his mouth movements that he had got to the plum stone and I wondered what he was going to do with it. I remember thinking: "Oh, God, I hope he doesn't spit it out."

'Almost at that moment he turned his head and spat the stone towards a large potted palm in a stoneware pot. It hit the pot making quite a large noise. Still, no one appeared to notice, and the conversation went on. His hands seemed to be covered in plum puree, where he had wrestled with the fruit before putting it to his mouth. Suddenly, Neil Kinnock turned to Maxwell and said he would like to introduce him to so and so. I watched in astonishment as Maxwell thrust out his great empurpled paw and the two men shook hands.'

Reporting Maxwell: Stories From Journalists

'Journalists on top, management on tap!' So said Robert Maxwell when he took over Mirror Group Newspapers. But, as so often in other areas of his life, what Robert Maxwell said didn't mean very much, though he may have believed his words at the time.

At a press conference to celebrate his takeover Maxwell boasted: 'Under my management editors will be free to produce their newspapers without interference with their journalistic skills and judgement.' Anyone who knew Maxwell knew that he would not be able to resist playing with his new toy. As one editor put it, editors who were summoned up to a dozen times a day by Maxwell wondered what real interference must be like!

He often demanded that meetings between him and foreign heads of state were given undue prominence in the papers. That was quite apart from the many campaigns he ran for which editorial space in the papers seemed to be one of the prime motivating forces. He phoned the *Daily Mirror* newsdesk with story ideas he wanted covered, but his influence didn't stop there. *Daily Mirror* reporter Bill Akass and photographer Kenny Lennox were out in the Arabian Gulf in the days leading up to the war watching the build-up of the allied forces.

'Before we left we were briefed by Bob Maxwell, who told us to contact a Mr Adjani, a representative of Maxwell's in the Gulf. In Dhahran, I was phoned by Adjani who asked us for personal introductions to US and British military commanders. I wasn't sure what it was about but I realized it was for commercial reasons, so I offered phone numbers but said I couldn't make introductions. I thought no more about it.

'Then, after a tiring trip into the desert, I rang the newsdesk and was told that Maxwell wanted to speak to me because I had been rude to someone. I rang Maxwell and decided to tape record our conversation. Maxwell accused me of failing to help Adjani and finally told me why he thought it was so important – he wanted me to make introductions so that Adjani could sell sets of encyclopaedias to the troops.

'I said to Maxwell: "Look, I'm here as a journalist, it will make me a laughing stock to do this." Maxwell shouted down the phone: "Don't be silly. I'll have to replace you."

'Then the line went dead. I wasn't replaced because the Editor of the *Mirror*, Roy Greenslade, stuck up for me. He told Maxwell that the paper couldn't be seen to have a reporter covering a war and selling encyclopaedias to the troops.'

*   *   *

When Maxwell took over Mirror Group Newspapers he promised the award-winning reporter John Pilger, that there would be no interference. Some hope!

'In January 1985 I was assigned to go to Bulgaria. Bulgaria? An appointment had been made for me to see the Bulgarian Ambassador in London, who would explain my assignment; he had recently been to the *Mirror* for lunch with the publisher.

'The Ambassador came to the point quickly. "Mr Maxwell tells me you will fly to Sofia next week and write the truth about the Pope affair," he said. The "Pope Affair" was the coming trial in Rome of a Turk who had attempted to assassinate the Pope and who had implicated three Bulgarians as part of an alleged plot by the Bulgarian KGB to kill the Pope on behalf of the Kremlin.

'I told the Ambassador I had not agreed to go to Bulgaria.

'He said: "But Mr Maxwell himself is going soon. And he says you are a good communist." I laughed and said that I was not a communist, good or bad, and that I had no intention of doing a whitewash job for the Bulgarian government.

'Back at the office I wrote a memorandum to Maxwell proposing that: "If the *Mirror* really wants to pursue the story, there seems to be only one way to go about it: to investigate all the available evidence from all sides – Italy, Bulgaria and Washington. I am sure it will be appreciated I do not wish to be associated with the Bulgarians at this stage. And I strongly recommend that the *Mirror* avoids any Bulgarian initiative on the Pope story."

'Shortly afterwards, in February 1985, Maxwell flew to Sofia accompanied by a *Daily Mirror* reporter and photographer. The report that followed in the *Mirror* might have been written by a Bulgarian PR man. It burbled enthusiastically about how the publisher had dined at

the court of a modest Communist King [who] brought forth caviar, then consommé, then soufflés, then veal. Vodka vied with brandy, white and red wines – with champagne twinkling through cut-glass crystal. But the 'king' leaned back and quietly ordered a swift light ale. When you're the Boss – and everyone knows it – you can do things like that.

Today Todor Zhivkov, President of Bulgaria, professional revolutionary and – after 30 years – the longest-serving leader in the Soviet bloc, was gently easing back the curtain on his iron image. 'I don't really approve of champagne,' he said. 'But we serve it for protocol's sake and to remind us when it's time to make speeches.'

He laughed softly and looked longingly back through thick, gold-rimmed glasses to his light ale. That jokey style last month bowled over Sir Geoffrey Howe, the first British Foreign Secretary to visit Bulgaria for more than 100 years. It contrasts clearly with his country's image as the heart of the Balkans, the Kremlin's stooge, infamous for poisoned umbrellas and the alleged plot to kill the Pope.

Not surprisingly it's an image the President indignantly dismisses as propaganda. Bulgaria for him should be seen by the West as a tourist top-spot, a go-ahead place with one of East Europe's most successful economies and virtually no foreign debt. Science, technology, profits and peace are his keys to Bulgaria's future. ...

'And so it went on until it reached the president's "special guest" across the table, Robert Maxwell, and got to the point:
"'The Mirror Group Publisher has just struck a huge deal with the Bulgarian Government to help update the country's printing and packaging industries."
'This report occupied half the *Mirror*'s centre pages and was illustrated by a picture of President Zhivkov and Robert Maxwell with their arms on each other. It was published on Monday, 4 March, the day after the end of the miners' strike, Britain's longest and most bitter industrial upheaval since the General Strike. Clearly, updating the printing and packaging industries in Bulgaria was considered more important.'

*   *   *

He used the papers to try and tone down any criticism of his friends, whether they were disgraced City figures or unpopular governments. Maxwell didn't confine himself to meddling in the affairs of his own newspapers. Wherever there was criticism of himself, he would challenge it, he used the full vigour of the libel laws.

Maxwell was so litigious that journalists and publishers thought twice about saying anything critical about him. However, although Maxwell began hundreds of actions, not many ever came to court. What is interesting is the sheer range of people he would attack if he felt challenged. Oxford Labour Party regularly received £500 from the local papers in settlement of libel writs which had been taken out after some unsatisfactory news report. The magazine *Private Eye* was sued on a number of occasions, once for deliberately mixing up a picture of Maxwell with one of the East End gangsters, the Kray twins.

Maxwell was spectacularly successful at times in obtaining damages. He won £55,000 from *Private Eye* for suggestions that he was paying political expenses in the hope of a peerage. He successfully stopped the publication of Thompson and Delano's book *Maxwell, a Portrait of Power*, winning both damages and the pulping of two editions. Against Tom Bower's book *Maxwell: The Outsider* he was less successful, but his threat to sue booksellers unless they gave an undertaking not to sell the unauthorized biographies cleared the books off all but the bravest booksellers' shelves. Many booksellers retaliated against Maxwell's bully-boy tactics by banishing Joe Haines's official biography of Maxwell, while the publishers Bantam Press and Aurum offered indemnity to any bookseller selling their books.

In a letter to the trade paper *Publishing News*, Maxwell admitted that 'Wealth is undoubtedly powerful. The libel laws are unquestionably a rich man's weapon.' One of Maxwell's lawyers told me that the publisher was not too worried about winning; what concerned him was that people should know that they could not get away with bad-mouthing him.

The reason why Maxwell was obsessed about keeping the lid on his affairs is now all too obvious: he had plenty to hide, and it was clearly against his interests for journalists to dig up information about his private life and business affairs. Even when critical material made it into print Maxwell and his team of experts would pour over it with a fine-tooth comb hoping to find small inaccuracies, which Maxwell would then get the offending newspaper to admit to and retract. In this way he rubbished many of the main findings of reporters or City analysts by nitpicking over small details which may have been difficult to verify in a notoriously secretive organization like the Maxwell media empire.

Publishers were brow-beaten into watering down any criticism of Maxwell by the threat of unending legal action and the huge costs that would entail. Journalists may have had their stories spiked, but the more secretive someone is and the more bullying their tactics, the more likely it is that each time a story is written and then watered down or not published, word gets around that the man really does have something to hide. So it was with Maxwell.

Of course, journalists are by nature worse gossips than washerwomen. There are very few exclusive stories because we find a good tale hard to keep to ourselves. This ensures circulation of a wealth of information, some reliable, some not, into which any investigator can dip. It also means that journalists tend to be a rich source of stories: they move in wide social circles, and can observe the 'great and the good' at work and play.

It has been suggested that Maxwell wanted to own newspapers so that he could stop people writing nasty things about him. The theory is implausible for two reasons: first, because, as a newspaper proprietor, you are automatically a target for rival newspapers; and, second, because the journalists you employ are bound to gossip about you with their friends on those rival papers.

*   *   *

Maxwell on more than one occasion described himself as 'a man who shuns publicity'. He shunned it so assiduously that he once spent $200,000 to sit next to Ronald Reagan at a dinner in California and have his photograph taken. Maxwell would – in his terms, justifiably – have regarded it as money well spent: such public relations 'scoops' enabled him to create the sort of public persona for which he yearned: he became Maxwell the multimillionaire; Maxwell the world statesman; Maxwell the man who saved this paper or that business; Maxwell the man who gave a fortune away to help

AIDS, or set up educational foundations or gave succour to the poor and needy. The smokescreen ultimately prevented few from seeing the real Robert Maxwell – the liar, the cheat and the thief.

*   *   *

Noel Lewis is a former BBC political correspondent who moved to the Mirror Group and worked there, as he puts it, for 'two years and one day'.

'Soon after joining the *Mirror* I was due to go to an EEC summit conference on the island of Rhodes. It was in December 1989. One day I was called into a staff meeting in the rarefied atmosphere of the ninth floor of Maxwell House – that's where all the big decisions were made. The meeting was due to be hosted by Peter Jay, and when I arrived there were about a dozen people standing around drinking coffee. Then Jay burst into the room and announced that "The Publisher" had instructed us to launch *The European* newspaper at the Rhodes conference. *The European* was nowhere near ready to be launched but we realized that Captain Bob wanted to go to the conference as a world figure. He believed that launching *The European* would help him achieve that ambition. An enormous press conference was to be organized and we were told that we all had to play our part. Peter Jay stressed the point that it was important for the moment that the plans be kept secret.

'He said: "In view of the historic nature of the site and in deference to our publisher, we will code-name this Operation Colossus." Remarkably no one laughed. (I later realized that reports of any laughter might have got back to Captain Bob, possibly placing our jobs at risk.)

'I wondered what sort of organization I had joined.'

*   *   *

The last controversy which surrounded Robert Maxwell was the one in which the American journalist Seymour Hersch claimed in his book *The Samson Option* that Maxwell was an agent of Mossad, the Israeli secret service. The allegation was based on information supplied by Ari Ben-Menasche, an Israeli, who himself claimed to be a former Mossad agent. Hersch believed Ben-Menasche's claim that in 1985 he and a Briton called Nick Davies secretly sold weapons to Iran with the backing of the then US Vice President, George Bush, and the Israeli Prime Minister, Yitzhak Shamir. Ben-Menasche claimed that, at the time of the arms sales, he didn't know that Nick Davies was a journalist with the *Daily Mirror*. In fact, Davies was the paper's Foreign Editor and often travelled the world with Maxwell.

Davies denied the Hersch allegations and Maxwell was said to be furious by what had been written about him. The publication of Hersch's book in October 1991 was quickly followed by writs alleging defamation on behalf of both Maxwell and Davies.

For a short but intense moment, the story grabbed public attention. Questions were asked in the House of Commons and the publishers of the Hersch book quickly flew the author to London, where he appeared before a packed news conference.

Robert Maxwell had described all of Hersch's allegations as 'ludicrous, a total invention'. He had accepted Davies's denials, especially the refutation of one critical suggestion by Hersch that Davies had visited Ohio in 1985 to buy arms. The *Mirror* stated that a letter which suggested Davies had visited Ohio for arms-dealing talks was a 'forgery'. Two days later the *Mirror*'s bitter rival, the *Sun*, published a photograph which proved Davies had indeed visited Ohio. Davies then apologized for a 'lapse of memory' and a few days later he was fired.

The whole saga took an even more dramatic turn when fresh allegations emerged that linked Maxwell with the kidnapping of Mordechai Vanunu, an Israeli who had leaked information to the *Sunday Times* about his country's secret nuclear bomb-making factory in the Negev desert. He had been lured away from Britain and was kidnapped by Mossad agents. He was eventually returned to Israel and is now serving a prison sentence.

Throughout this trying time Nick Davies kept his counsel, and was writing his own version of events. Despite what happened he has many fond memories of Robert Maxwell.

'In 1989 I went to Finland with Maxwell. He had a meeting with the Finnish Prime Minister (whose name I cannot remember). The meeting went on for an hour. At the end of it the Prime Minister said: "I thoroughly enjoyed my meeting with Robert Maxwell, but I wish he would allow me to say a word or two."'

At one time Maxwell employed Senator John Tower, once a presidential contender, who later died in a plane crash. The tallest thing about Senator Tower was his name, and Nick Davies suggests the senator was little more than five feet in height. He was particularly sensitive about his stature, a sensitivity which, according to Nick Davies, found little sympathy in Robert Maxwell.

'Maxwell was on board his yacht the *Lady Ghislaine* in New York. He was having a party and as usual had invited everybody who was anybody in the United States. Senator Tower was among the guests. As everyone probably knows by now, Maxwell insisted that all guests aboard the yacht, without exception, had to take their shoes off before going below deck in order to protect his expensive carpets.

'Senator Tower begged for dispensation. He had cuban heels on and was afraid that without them his true height would be revealed. Maxwell rejected his request and for the whole evening there was this comic spectacle of Senator Tower going around mingling with the guests while standing on tip-toe.'

*   *   *

Maxwell's takeover of Mirror Group Newspapers happened right in the middle of the miners' strike – the longest-running industrial dispute in Britain this century. Maxwell believed that this strike was damaging to the whole Labour movement and saw himself as the man who could solve it. One Saturday afternoon he phoned John Pilger's home.

'He told me to arrange a "secret" meeting with the miners' union President, Arthur Scargill (whom I had never met, although I had many links with the miners). I did not like the role of fixer; but the miners needed every ally they could get and, more important, their case urgently needed a fair hearing in a national newspaper. The meeting was to be held near the NUM headquarters in Sheffield, preferably in a hotel with a heliport on it or nearby, as the publisher wanted to arrive and leave by this form of transport. This did not seem to me commensurate with secrecy. Nevertheless, a bemused Peter Heathfield, the NUM's General Secretary, suggested the Hallam Tower Hotel, which is on the edge of a wood outside Sheffield. It did not have a heliport, he said, but Sheffield had an airport.

'The *Mirror* "team" was Maxwell, Robert Edwards (then Editor of the *Sunday Mirror* and a long-standing trustee of the publisher), Geoffrey Goodman, the *Mirror*'s Industrial Editor, Joe Haines, MGN Political Editor, and myself. I received several phone calls from the publisher's personal assistant about the availability of "No. 1" and "No. 2" helicopter and whether the smaller one could accommodate us all. I said I would prefer to travel by train (which, anyway, was faster).

'At the news-stand at St Pancras Station the front page of the *Daily Mirror* was triumphant:

ONLY in the *Mirror*
The *REAL* £million
Here it is – the *Mirror*'s REAL £1 million. IN CASH.

And tax free to the winner of our Win a £Million game in Mirror Group Newspapers. MGN Publisher Robert Maxwell saw a million in banknotes for the first time yesterday. He admitted he was impressed and beamed: 'I'm itching to give it to one of our readers.' He went on:

'This is it – one million in cash which will make someone a millionaire.'

Mr Maxwell's pretty daughter, Ghislaine, 22, was on hand to see the cash. Ghislaine said: 'It pleases me to know it will make one of our readers happy.'

'Dominating the front page was a large picture of Robert Maxwell leaning on a trolley loaded with a million pounds in bundles of various denominations. I was admiring this when a familiar baritone boomed over my shoulder: "Well, what do you think of it?"

'It was my publisher, no less, attended by Robert Edwards; both helicopters had been grounded by fog and the three of us would now journey together to Sheffield. Goodman had gone by car; Haines had been assigned to wait for the helicopter, so that the publisher could fly back in it.

'Maxwell was clearly delighted with a front page on which there were images only of himself and money. He held it up and seemed to be reading the few words on it again and again. When the British Rail waiter serving us breakfast showed interest Maxwell said: "Do you want us to sign it? Yes, of course you do; it'll be a collector's item."

'The waiter seemed grateful, though perplexed, especially when the publisher opened his attaché case and passed around one of the bundles of £50 notes which had appeared in the front-page picture. Edwards and I were invited to hold it, then return it.

'On the way to Sheffield Maxwell spoke about his "deep concerns" – the need for propriety and self-discipline "in the country". The young, above all, lacked this discipline; standards had fallen; selfishness was rampant. And everything was linked: drug-taking, violence on the football terraces, violence on the picket lines. A new commitment to morality was needed, a new patriotism.

'The meeting in the penthouse of the Hallam Tower lasted almost four hours, during which Arthur Scargill and Peter Heathfield, with patience, skill and sustained good humour, laid out the miners' case, explaining why the union could not agree to closing pits on ill-defined "uneconomic" grounds. They based their argument on an agreement in the 1974 Plan for Coal which allowed closures only when coal reserves were exhausted. They showed us evidence of the Coal Board's manipulation of the Colliery Review Procedure and of the union's attempts to compromise, few of which had received national publicity.

'For his part, Maxwell told them of his "fears for the country": of a "breakdown in law and order and civilized values" and the spectre of revolution on the streets. It was up to them to prevent this, he said. As the afternoon wore on, the miners' case – the destruction of communities, the need to keep open the coalfields as North Sea oil dwindled, the burden on society of tens of thousands of redundant miners, the duplicity of the Coal Board under its Thatcher-appointed chairman Ian MacGregor – seemed increasingly irrelevant to the real purpose of the meeting; and at times a certain incredulity would slip across the faces of Heathfield and Scargill as they were lectured, now incessantly, on their "responsibilities to the nation".

'The next morning I phoned Maxwell and said that we had been given at the meeting substantial evidence that the Coal Board and the Government were not telling half the truth about their dealings with the miners, and that the *Mirror* ought to run the story. I proposed that I write it. "You mustn't be taken in," said Maxwell. "I'll get Haines to do a leader." However, he did authorize a major piece by me about police violence in the coalfields, which was one of the issues that Scargill had raised at the meeting: an indication both of Maxwell's quixotic temperament and his assumption of the role of editor.

'I was not on Maxwell's "team" three weeks later when he met Scargill at Brighton during the Trades Union Congress. Maxwell was in his element. Following the "secret" negotiations that the *Mirror* had trumpeted each day, Maxwell, in shirt sleeves, gave impromptu press conferences on the seafront. He was merely offering his "good offices" he said, and doing what had to be done in the national interest. Shortly afterwards, on 10 September, Maxwell's efforts in the national interest seemed to have paid off. The *Mirror*'s front page read:

SCARGILL TO BALLOT MINERS
ON FINAL OFFER
by Terry Pattinson

Peace talks aimed at settling the miners' strike ended after only two hours last night.

But the *Mirror* can exclusively reveal that whatever the outcome, miners will be asked to vote on the Coal Board's final offer.

Both sides were non-committal last night. ...

'On page 2 the *Mirror*'s revelation was described as an "astonishing development" and there were several columns of detail about the "final package". This second story was "by a special correspondent".

'Almost none of it was true. Terry Pattinson, the *Mirror*'s respected industrial reporter, had indeed filed from Scotland that "peace talks had ended after only two hours" and that "both sides were non-committal". This much was true. The second paragraph, in which "the *Mirror* can exclusively reveal" that the miners were to hold a ballot, was inserted into his copy, and the first he heard about his "scoop" was when he returned home the next morning and was congratulated by his wife. The night before, the *Mirror*'s wire room had received a telex message directly from Maxwell House, the head offices of Pergamon Press which owns Mirror Group Newspapers. There was no name on the telex, which was marked "MUST". Assuming it was sent by Maxwell, *Mirror* executives decided to publish it. A leader, written by Joe Haines, entitled "A vote for sanity" and lauding the non-existent decision to ballot, was published alongside it. The identity of the "special correspondent" was not revealed.'

*   *   *

Everyone who ever had any dealings with Robert Maxwell was at one time or another kept waiting. Those who didn't know him took it personally but in fact he treated everybody, from the highest to the lowest, in exactly the same way.

Patrick Forbes was a director with Thames Television in 1989 when he was sent with a reporter, cameraman and sound recordist to interview the publisher for Thames Television's *City Programme*. They spent two hours waiting to see Maxwell.

'Eventually we told the PR man that we couldn't hang around any longer and within minutes we were ushered into Maxwell's private office on the tenth floor of Maxwell House. It appeared to be empty and we assumed we had been let in to set up the camera and adjust the lighting. Then, suddenly, from somewhere in the room – we couldn't tell where – came the Vesuvian rumblings of someone on the toilet. This awful noise went on for several minutes. Eventually a bookcase of false books opened and out stepped Robert Maxwell. He didn't speak but came over to us and sat down in front of the camera as if nothing had happened.'

A similar experience awaited Jenni Frazer, a senior journalist with the *Jewish Chronicle*, when she interviewed Maxwell in 1986.

'Setting up the interview took 15 months. Eventually Maxwell agreed to see me. When we went into his private offices at the top of Maxwell House, Maxwell was in the bathroom. He was on the toilet and had left the door open. We couldn't see him, but we could hear him. It was disgusting. But I believe it was psychologically important to him. He was letting us know that he didn't have to behave nicely because it wasn't necessary to impress us.

'We had wanted to interview Maxwell to get the definitive word on Maxwell and the Jews. We wanted finally to find out how he felt about being Jewish. After all, in 1964, he had written to the *Jewish Chronicle* to tell us that he was "now a member of the Church of England". But quite recently he'd begun to be actively involved in charitable work with Anglo-Jewry and had supported Israel.

'However, when he came out of the bathroom he didn't want to answer any of my questions about his Jewishness. He told me he didn't want to waste time and so he'd got some material together for me. I got a potted biography, a hardback book about the rise and rise of Oxford United, a press release about his purchase of British Airways Helicopters and another press release to say he'd become president of the new European Satellite Television Consortium.

'Then he said: "I have only two things I want to tell you that are of interest to the Jewish community." He then told me that because of ignorance about the Holocaust he was launching a *Holocaust Studies Journal* and that there would be an international conference on the Holocaust in two years' time. "That's all I have to say – unless there's anything you want to ask me?"

'I remember trying to ask him about why he had suddenly become associated with the Jewish community, and whether he believed that criticism of him might be based on anti-semitism. But he fended off the questions, only insisting: "I certainly consider myself Jewish – I was born Jewish and I shall die Jewish."'

This interview had been sought because Maxwell's Jewishness had been a considerable source of controversy for nearly 30 years. In 1964 the *Jewish Chronicle* was updating the *Jewish Year Book* and had approached those newly elected MPs that it believed might be Jewish and asked them if they would mind being listed in the year book. Maxwell's statement about belonging to the Church of England was a response to this. It dogged Maxwell's footsteps for the rest of his life – so much so that in June 1988 his wife felt she had to write to the *Jewish Chronicle* newspaper to clarify the position. Mrs Maxwell said that her husband denied being Jewish in 'a prankish telephone call made as a joke to your paper 25 years ago, to get rid of a badgering reporter'. She went on to say: 'My husband never became a member of any Christian church. I should know: I am his Christian wife.'

So how did this misunderstanding begin? Let's go to the man who took the original call from Maxwell back in 1964. David Kessler is former chairman and managing director of the *Jewish Chronicle* newspaper:

'It was when he was first elected to Parliament. The Editor of the *Jewish Year Book* was updating his list of Jewish MPs. A form was sent to Maxwell to fill in, but instead of filling it in he called me up. He told me he'd received this letter from the *Jewish Year Book* but said: "You know I'm not Jewish."

'I was surprised and said that everyone imagined he was. He said he was born a Jew but added, "I was married in Church so I am no longer Jewish."

'I told him that had nothing to do with it. I said if he didn't want to be included on the list of Jewish MPs that was one thing, but that the majority of people would regard him as Jewish. I told him not to be so stupid as to deny his origins and added: "I think you are making a grave mistake to give the impression you are not Jewish when everybody knows you've got Jewish origins."

'I got the impression that he was responding in the way that many central European Jews have done: in denying their religion so that they could get on in the world. Some would even have themselves baptized. But I reminded him that this was England and that here people preferred others to be honest about their origins, however humble they might be.'

Over the years Maxwell did become more and more involved with Jewish causes and was a staunch supporter of the state of Israel. He gave two million dollars to a drive for Israeli bonds in 1988, and then said: 'I always say yes. If I were a woman, I would always be pregnant.'

*　　*　　*

John Jackson, a *Daily Mirror* reporter, heard how one man who had been kept waiting for hours managed to get to see Maxwell.

'He realized that the only person who appeared to have unlimited access to the Publisher was our leader writer, who came up in the evening to show Mr Maxwell the leader (the paper's comment column) for the next day. 'This man went in on the coat-tails of the leader writer, saying he was with him. He met Maxwell and his whole entourage coming out and said: "Ah, Mr Maxwell, my name is Mr. ..."

'Maxwell looked at him and asked: "Have you ever been up in a helicopter?"

'The man didn't have time to reply before Maxwell followed up with: "Well, you are going up in one now." This bloke finished up travelling in Maxwell's helicopter all the way to Leeds because Maxwell was recording something at YTV. Then, because Maxwell wasn't coming back to London immediately he managed to hitch a ride in David Frost's plane. I don't know whether he ever got what he wanted, but I doubt it.'

Another long waiter was BBC Radio reporter Phil Jones:

'I was sent out by Radio 4's *Today* programme to interview Mr Maxwell, who'd taken over the Mirror Group of newspapers about a year before.

'He kept me waiting for two hours on the ninth floor of Maxwell House – that's the floor below the penthouse suite. I was furious! Eventually I phoned the Editor of the programme, who told me to hang on for another half an hour. When that time had passed with no sign of my interview, I spoke to Mr Maxwell's PR man and told him that was it – I was going. But he asked me to wait, because Maxwell would see me at once.

'I did the interview, though I can't even remember what it was about now. At the end I thanked Maxwell. He then asked me if I had read his book about the *Private Eye* libel case, which he thought should be mandatory reading for all journalists.

'"Would you like a copy?" he asked.

'"That would be kind," I replied.

'"Get Mr Jones a copy of my book!" Robert Maxwell barked at his press officer.

'I asked him if he would sign it. "Certainly!"

'I explained that I was going out with a young lady, and would he write "Best wishes for the New Year" as well as his signature. He did so and then asked me if she would read the book.

'I said: "I'm sure she will – she's got a great sense of humour," and turned to leave the room.

'As I reached the door he bellowed after me: "She must have to be going out with you!"'

Daily Mirror reporter Don MacKay first met Maxwell when he worked on the ill-fated Glasgow *Daily News*, the paper formed by a workers' co-operative in 1975 after Beaverbrook Newspapers closed the Scottish *Daily Express*. When the *Daily News* failed, Don MacKay (with a wife and baby daughter) had to find work quickly and took a job on a paper in Northamptonshire. The constituency of Buckingham was on Don's patch and he suggested to his news editor that they spend a day with the prospective parliamentary candidate, Robert Maxwell.

'My bosses warmed to the idea of profiling Robert Maxwell and had suggested that my wife and I take him and his wife out to dinner.

'I phoned Maxwell and he said only he would be able to make it. He asked me if I had booked a restaurant. When I said I hadn't he suggested that he should book it. Since he knew the area better than I did, it seemed a good idea. We set a time and date and he told me he would send a car to collect me. At the appointed time his Rolls Royce appeared and took us to the restaurant.

'Maxwell was sitting at a table surrounded by waiters in a room completely empty of other guests. He informed us that he had indeed booked the restaurant; he had booked the whole restaurant and added that he insisted on paying. We had a pleasant meal and drank a lot. Maxwell seemed to enjoy my wife's company and asked about our family.

We told him we were worried about our daughter's eyesight. She had been born with a defect and it appeared that there was no means of curing it.

'At the end of the meal Maxwell sent us home in the Rolls Royce. But going through the winding country lanes I began to feel sick. When we pulled up outside my home I was sick all down the driver's headrest.

'The next day I went to work feeling a little fragile. As I approached the office I noticed Maxwell's Rolls Royce outside. I said good morning to the driver and apologized. He said he'd spent half the night cleaning up the mess. When I went inside I was informed that the newspaper editor and the company's Chairman wanted to see me in the Chairman's office. I thought Maxwell must have complained about my being sick in his car and that I was going to get the sack. I walked in; the editor and the Chairman were talking to Maxwell.

'I immediately said that I supposed that they wanted me to clear my desk. They all looked perplexed. Then the Chairman explained that Mr Maxwell had called after having heard about the problems with my little girl's eyesight. He had arranged for her to see a Harley Street specialist at no cost to me and later paid for her to have an operation in a private hospital, again at no cost to me. At no time in the future did he ever ask for anything in return, nor did he ever remind me of his kindness.

'My daughter is now 17 and her eyesight has been fully restored.'

*   *   *

During Maxwell's reign at the *Mirror* he often rang the newsdesk and asked: 'What's cooking?' The hapless employee who happened to pick up the phone at whatever time of day or night it was would be expected to supply a rundown of the important story which the *Mirror* was running to ground. As everyone who has worked in journalism will know, on many occasions there is nothing going on. This answer wouldn't satisfy the Publisher, who would simply repeat his question.

On one occasion he rang the newsdesk during the evening and bellowed 'What's cooking?' The journalist at the other end of the receiver couldn't think of anything, but had been watching the television news and had seen pictures from the Italian port of Bari, which was having to cope with an influx of Albanian refugees. He described to the Chairman how moving these pictures had been, with human beings clinging like limpets to every piece of overloaded metal. The Chairman listened to his employee's moving description. Then there was a long pause. Eventually Maxwell said: 'F..k the Albanians!' and the phone went dead.

Maxwell's level of compassion often appeared to be measured by how much publicity he could gain for himself by being involved in good causes. His aid for Ethiopia campaign is a case in point. He flew into the famine-stricken country himself and was filmed dishing out food. Before he left he'd been photographed with Lord King, Chairman of British Airways, who were laying on free transport. Maxwell had left instructions at the *Mirror* that a picture of him setting off on his mercy mission was to be displayed prominently on page one. In the end it was cut down drastically and appeared only as a head and shoulders shot. Insiders at the *Mirror* say this was because he had spilt something down the front of his trousers which had left a huge stain. Maxwell was furious when he found out that his instructions had been disobeyed – and no one at the *Mirror* had the courage to tell him the truth.

Maxwell was a bully and like most bullies he had a keen eye for victims. He attacked those who showed fear and gave a grudging respect to those that stood up to him. During his famine-relief visit to Ethiopia he held a meeting at the Addis Hilton.

'Is everyone here feeling well?' Maxwell inquired.

'Actually, I'm not feeling too good, Mr Maxwell,' a middle aged PR man on Captain Bob's staff replied.

'Your problem,' Maxwell diagnosed, 'is that you've got big jobbies! What have you got?'

The PR man was too embarrassed to reply. However, Maxwell had gained the attention of the entire room, which was probably what he wanted in the first place, and he pressed on: 'I've just asked you – what have you got?'

The PR man looked miserable. There was still no answer.

Once more Maxwell put the question, this time his tone even more menacing: 'Answer me! What have you got?'

Finally the PR man mumbled: 'I've got big ... jobbies.'

Satisfied, Maxwell continued with the meeting.

*   *   *

Maxwell also liked to be seen to be generous. It seems that he was particularly fond of giving away cars for a pound. The most celebrated example of this was when he gave former Tory cabinet minister, Peter Walker, a £50,000 Mercedes car for the price of a pound coin.

Others also acquired a company car for a pound. On one occasion, according to legend, Maxwell sacked a journalist who, angry at his treatment, demanded to see him. The outraged hack told staff in the car park at the *Mirror* HQ that Maxwell would be forced to reconsider. But when the reporter emerged from Maxwell's eyrie all he had was a piece of paper authorizing the garage staff to sell the company car allocated to that reporter on payment of one pound. This was duly done. Five minutes later Maxwell is said to have phoned down and tried to have his authorization cancelled, but it was too late.

On another occasion a car Maxwell gave away for a pound was later discovered to have been leased from a car hire firm!

Finally, one Christmas, Maxwell gave Harry Harris, his favourite football reporter, a new BMW, while Mrs Harris received the biggest bouquet of flowers ever seen. Harry Harris said he couldn't accept the gift and that, in any case, he couldn't drive. But Maxwell refused to take his present back.

Another car story concerns Jean Baddeley, at one time Robert Maxwell's personal assistant and probably the person closer to Maxwell than anyone in his working life. (According to Maxwell's will she is to receive £100,000 and have her job guaranteed for life.) Jean had always wanted a Porsche car and Maxwell told executives at Mirror Group Newspapers that he had thought of buying her one. Lord Kearton, former chairman of the Industrial Reorganization Corporation and non-executive chairman of the British Printing Corporation before Maxwell took it over, takes up the story.

'A big party was being held at the *Mirror* after the general election of 1987. There was always a post-election party – it goes back to the days of Cecil King – and Maxwell was just keeping up with the tradition. It had nothing much to do with politics and was just an excuse for a party. At this particular event Maxwell had decided to honour his secretary, Jean Baddeley, who had been with him for years. He told everyone that he would have liked to buy her a Porsche car but that money was a little difficult at the time. So he said he was buying her a large cake with a Porsche made out of marzipan. He presented her with the cake at the party and although she was gracious I could see she was very disappointed.

'Then he said to her: "Come outside, Jean. I do have a small present for you."

'The real Porsche was of course waiting there for her. I thought that was really sweet.'

When political correspondent Noel Lewis joined MGN he, too, thought he was entitled to a car. 'When some time had elapsed and there was no sign of my car I approached Joe Haines about it. He said Maxwell didn't like giving away cars and insisted on knowing about any expenditure over £500, which surprised me for a man of his supposed immense wealth. Joe said that he would have to get him in a good mood before asking him about my car.

'I was also surprised that Joe Haines couldn't authorize a car for me. After all, he was Political Editor. Under normal circumstances he could appoint people so I had expected that he could supply them with a motor car, too.

'Then Joe explained how we had to be patient. He illustrated this with the tale of another senior executive who had 12 people working under him and kept pressing for their cars to be traded in and for them to be supplied with new ones. Haines told me that eventually Maxwell did look at the request. After some deliberation he decided that not only did they not need 12 new cars: they also didn't need the 12 jobs that went with them. They all got the sack.

'After that I decided to let Joe do the negotiating and eventually I got my car.'

*   *   *

John Naughton, Television Critic of the *Observer* (and 1991's Newspaper Critic of the Year) met Robert Maxwell only once, but the 'larger-than-life character' made an indelible impression. The occasion was a lunch Maxwell gave for columnists and editorial staff on the *London Daily News* shortly before the paper was launched. It was the day that Prince Edward quit the Royal Marines.

'Upon arrival in the Publisher's Office at the top of the *Mirror* building, we were ushered by a butler into "Maxwell House" – the unique blend of Louis Quatorze and Southfork decor which was Captain Bob's London home. Cocktails were served to the assembled guests by servants in an atmosphere which resembled, in its hushed propriety, the prelude to a public hanging.

'After a time a pair of double doors were thrown open and our host appeared. He went round shaking hands and saying: "How do you do? I'm Robert Maxwell", as if there might be some doubt about his identity. Then he looked round the company disdainfully, seeking someone worthy of his attention. His gaze alighted on Ken Livingstone, then at the height of his fame. Maxwell motioned brusquely to him, much as one might summon a recalcitrant dog, and walked out of the room, followed by an obedient Livingstone. The rest of us talked quietly among ourselves.

'After a while, the great man reappeared and invited us to join him for "luncheon". This old fashioned locution, by the way, seemed to be typical of his speech, at least when he was trying to be polite. On my way in I had passed him in a corridor, deep in conversation with two besuited lackeys. I caught a phrase as we went by: "We should issue proceedings forthwith," he said. His English sounded oddly quaint, as if he had learned it out of that mythical phrasebook in which the postilion has been struck by lightning.

'Lunch was served in the dining room where Cecil King used to plan his abortive coups against Harold Wilson. To my relief I found myself seated way below the salt and settled down to enjoy a quiet lunch. The food was excellent; the drink even better. Perhaps, I thought, there really was such a thing as a free lunch. Or at any rate a free luncheon.

'But it wasn't to be. Maxwell thumped the table and boomed: "Ladies and gentlemen, I invited you here not only to make your acquaintance but also to ascertain from you what you think my new paper should stand for. So I shall expect you to sing for your suppers.

'"And I shall start with you, Julian," he said, turning to a startled Julian Critchley, MP, who happened to be seated at his left. The parliamentarian murmured some elegant platitudes and passed the parcel to his neighbour who in turn uttered some high-minded sentiments. The paper should be truthful, should not invade people's privacy, should be entertaining to read, and so on. Mr Maxwell nodded his vigorous agreement with these banal propositions. I noticed that he had an unnerving habit of repeating every fifth word of what people said to him. It was probably his way of being polite but it made him sound slightly batty.

'This went on all round the table, each succeeding guest embellishing a portrait of a newspaper which was to be the publishing equivalent of Caesar's wife. By the time my turn came I was too drunk and bored to conform.

'"The purpose of a newspaper," I said pompously, "is to make trouble."

'At this a hush fell on the company.

'"How do you mean trouble?" asked mine host.

'"Well," I said, "first of all, trouble for the government."

'He nodded.

'"Then, trouble for the City of London."

'Again, he nodded.

'"And thirdly," I said, thinking it was as well to be hung for a sheep as for a lamb, "trouble for its proprietor."

'At this, all that could be heard was the terrified whimpering of *Mirror* executives who had taken up defensive positions under the table.

'"Would you care to explain?" asked Maxwell, in a voice of bottled thunder.

'"Well," I said, "if I'd been writing my column today I'd have said that it was high time British society decided whether a spell in the Royal Marines was a fit training for a chimpanzee, never mind a Prince of the Blood."

'Maxwell then gave me forcibly to understand that if I had tried to say such a thing in his newspaper he would have been Very Greatly Displeased. Indeed, he would have spiked it.

'At this, Magnus Linklater, the wretched Editor of the ill-fated but at this time embryonic newspaper – emitted a noise somewhere between a yelp and a gasp. But, flushed with excitement – not to mention Château Lynch-Bages '75 – I was beyond redemption, even by a solicitous and humane editor. I requested an explanation of the proprietor's repressive position.

'"It is one thing," boomed Maxwell, "for an unknown journalist like you to say such things. But if I were to publish such a column it would be tantamount to giving a message to the Youth of This Country that it is acceptable to renege on a commitment the moment the going gets tough."

'I sat there speechless, flabbergasted at the pomposity of the man. The rest of the company studied their fingernails while surreptitiously plotting the line to the nearest exit.

Silence reigned. Eventually another guest – Ms (now Lady) Tessa Blackstone – spoke: "Bullshit, Bob," she said.

'I have admired that lady ever since.'

*   *   *

There was a strike at the British Printing Corporation which had affected the publication of the *Radio Times*. BBC Radio reporter Phil Jones was sent along to interview Maxwell to find out what progress was being made in the dispute. Maxwell had a suite of private offices at BPC and Jones was shown up there by a public relations man.

'When Robert Maxwell walked into the room he seemed surprised to see me sitting in his private sanctum. He demanded to know what I was doing there. Since I didn't want to drop the PR man in it, I explained that I was a BBC reporter and was there to find out if there'd been any progress about the strike.

'"You've arrived at the right time," he said. "I'm just about to solve the dispute! In the meantime, would you like a drink?"

'"I think I could manage a gin and tonic," I replied.

'"Fetch the man a gin and tonic!" he told one of his staff. "And keep 'em coming!" Then Maxwell went away for about half an hour. When he returned he told me he had the story and gave me the details. I asked him for a phone to put over the copy. But the whole time I was phoning through the story he kept on interrupting and telling me how it should be written.

'In the end I said: "Thank you for your hospitality, Mr Maxwell, but I can write the story myself!" For some reason he seemed hurt by this and went off in a huff.'

*   *   *

Columnist John Smith of *The People* wrote the 'Man of the People' column. A few months before Robert Maxwell disappeared off the back of his yacht, one of Smith's most supportive readers died, at 90 years of age, and bequeathed his house to the 'Man of the People' column. Maxwell heard about this windfall and told Smith that he intended to knock down the house and build a block of flats on the site. Smith indicated to the publisher that the property wasn't his to dispose of as he wanted, but that it had been bequeathed to the 'Man of the People'.

Maxwell expostulated: 'But I *am* the Man of the People!'

The dispute over this bequest was still unresolved at the time of Maxwell's death.

*   *   *

Maxwell once told Joe Haines that 'everyone who works for me has total security.' When Haines pointed out that Maxwell was always sacking people he responded: 'Yes, but they are ex-employees and as such have no security at all.'

Maxwell was always hiring and firing on a whim. Roy Greenslade became Editor of the *Daily Mirror* in the early months of 1990. Less than six months later the job was offered to Joe Haines, who turned it down. One morning Haines was told by Maxwell that he still intended to sack Greenslade and that there would be an advertisement in the papers for the Editor's job. Shortly afterwards Maxwell told Haines he was glad he hadn't sacked Greenslade: he had now changed his mind and they were going to be 'friends for ever'. Maxwell then asked Haines if he was busy and said that if he wasn't he should come up and have lunch with him. Half an hour later Haines arrived at the ninth floor to have lunch with the Publisher and was told that Maxwell had decided to sack Greenslade after all.

*   *   *

There is no denying that inside the Mirror building Maxwell was a despotic ruler. Shortly after he took over, he instituted editorial lunches every Tuesday. Maxwell described those assembled as his 'cabinet'. (Insiders said that 'politburo' would have been a more appropriate term.)

At one of the think-tank meetings at which Maxwell was not present, someone asked Joe Haines if he now felt secure

at MGN. He said that he was so secure he was buying a
weekly season ticket. A few minutes later, when Haines
returned to the newsroom, Maxwell was able to repeat the
comment to him. Haines, not surprisingly, thought this was
sinister. However, considering Maxwell's methods, his ability
to 'discover' information is easily understandable.

In the early days Maxwell had an unrivalled reputation as
a union negotiator. Even the unions admitted it. But he
always gave himself whatever edge was possible. The large
dining room in his private penthouse apartment on the ninth
floor of Maxwell House was electronically bugged. It was
there that the union representatives would be assembled
before meeting Maxwell to negotiate. They would return
there at lunchtime or during other breaks in the discussions.
It's not surprising that they discussed amongst themselves
what they hoped to achieve and what progress they were
making. It is against this background that Maxwell's talents
as a negotiator should be assessed. In recent years his bugging
activities were extended to the phones of his company executives. Maxwell no doubt enjoyed using the information he
gained but he also liked the idea of knowing secrets – it was
all part of the power game to him.

Maxwell went to great lengths to protect his reputation as
a man who was tough on the unions. Steve Clarke, then a
reporter for Thames Television, remembers a revealing incident: 'It's some time ago now, but as I remember it, I had
to go down to Maxwell House with a television crew to
interview Robert Maxwell. One of the print unions had been
in dispute with Maxwell and had recently been fined £100,000
by the courts. The rumour was that Maxwell had himself
paid their fine. The union representative, Tony Dubbins, had
said officially that he couldn't comment but he had smiled
and added that the rumours weren't "a million miles from
the truth".

'Everyone believed it was Maxwell who had paid. So when
I got a chance to interview him, I put the theory to him. He
categorically denied it.

'I was sure he was lying. I mean, I have interviewed many people before and since, and some of them have clearly been evading the truth in their answers to questions. But I have never interviewed anyone whom I thought was simply lying to me except Robert Maxwell. When someone does that to you, what can you say? If you have no evidence to back your suspicion, all you can do is put the question again. But if, like Maxwell, they simply stare straight at you and lie, there is very little you can do. But it made me wonder what else he was capable of lying about.'

*   *   *

The extent and type of Maxwell's contacts and deals in Eastern Europe and the Soviet Union will probably never be known for sure. But, in any case, the image was probably more important than the reality.

John Miller, an expert on the Soviet Union, who formerly wrote for the *Daily Telegraph*, told this tale:

'The story goes back to the mid-1980s – I think it was 1984. I was a member of an organization called the Great Britain-USSR Association (it has since been renamed the Russia-Britain Centre). Anyway, they used to invite Soviet worthies over to this country to speak to the association. It was all paid for by the Foreign Office.

'On this particular occasion a Soviet journalist, Vsevelod Ovchinnikov, was the invited speaker. He had been correspondent for *Pravda* in both London and Tokyo and regarded himself as an expert on Britain and Japan. Anyway, he suddenly disappeared for a couple of days while in Britain. I had met him before and was due to sit in on a discussion with him in the office of Bill Deedes, then Editor of the *Daily Telegraph*. Ovchinnikov arrived and Deedes was pouring drinks for everyone when the phone rang. I heard him say, in a rather annoyed tone, "Oh, very well, send him up." He then turned to me and said: "It's bloody Maxwell. The front desk have told me he is coming up the stairs."

'Almost before he'd said it, in came Maxwell. "Hello,

Bill," he boomed, and then turned to Ovchinnikov and said: "Vsevelod, how are you? I hope Bill is looking after you?"

'It was as if it was Maxwell's office, not the office of the Editor of the *Daily Telegraph*. There then followed a discussion about events in the Soviet Union. The *Pravda* man gave us the party line, but it quickly became apparent that Maxwell knew more about Soviet policy than Ovchinnikov did. Maxwell told us of his contacts inside the USSR, bragged about the people he knew, how he was a close confident of Brezhnev and said that those he didn't know were not worth knowing. It was Maxwell at his best.

'Then he suddenly stood up and said: "Well, come along Vsevelod, we have to go to the theatre." He turned to us and explained that Ovchinnikov was his guest in London and he had to look after him. I knew this was a lie, that he was in fact a guest of the Great Britain-USSR Association, and that they had wondered what had become of him over the last couple of days.

'Bill Deedes asked me to see them off the premises. He said he didn't want them to get lost. What he really meant was he didn't want Maxwell nosing around the *Daily Telegraph* building pinching ideas. So I went downstairs with Maxwell and Ovchinnikov. Maxwell's Rolls Royce was parked on the pavement outside the building. As he was getting into the car I asked Maxwell what his interest in *Pravda* was.

'He said: "You never know, one day I might want to buy it and Ovchinnikov here might be my editor." He never did buy *Pravda*, although he did set up *Moscow News*. But I have always wondered if there was any truth in what he said or whether or not it was just another piece of his own image-making.'

*   *   *

John Jackson, a senior reporter on the *Daily Mirror*, worked closely with Maxwell on a number of occasions. He accompanied Mrs Maxwell and Philip Maxwell when they flew to the Canary Islands to identify Robert Maxwell's body. Jackson was told the news half an hour before it was released to news-gathering organizations and was with the family when they were helicoptered from the top of the *Mirror* building to Maxwell's private jet and on to the Canaries. He was impressed with how calm Mrs Maxwell and her son were and said that Philip's grasp of Spanish proved invaluable (he is married to an Argentinian).

Jackson stayed on the *Lady Ghislaine* and flew with the body to Jerusalem for the burial. He remembers the problems the family had in finding a coffin large enough for the publisher's body and that the private jet was too small to accommodate it. Eventually another plane was flown in; the coffin only just squeezed through the hatch into the cargo hold. (At one point it was suggested that the only way it would go in would be upright. A voice was heard to say that Mr Maxwell was beyond caring whether he stood up or lay down on the flight to Jerusalem.)

Jackson's close association with the publisher included working on his book *Malice in Wonderland*, the account of Maxwell's libel victory over the magazine *Private Eye*.

'During his action against *Private Eye* it was my task to keep him informed of progress from the court. On one occasion he was in New York, but he still wanted an up to the minute report. So he arranged for a satellite telephone link from a LandRover parked behind the High Court in Carey Street. The development that day was very complex and difficult to explain. But on the telephone I did my best. He asked for my opinion and I said I thought it was one battle lost.

'"Who is my solicitor?" he asked.

'"He's here if you want a word with him," I replied.

'He said "Put him on."

'His only words to the poor man were "You're fired!"

'After the libel action was won, Maxwell called a number of his staff together and swore them to secrecy. He told them he was going to produce a book about the case; they would have to work around the clock because it would have to be publishcd in three weeks.

'Macdonalds were going to publish the book and since he owned them that was really in-house. He told us that we were to have the run of the place: anything we wanted would be available. We were allocated the room next to his. But he said that for the time being not a soul must know of our plans. He emphasized this a number of times.

'Then one of his assistants came in and told him that there was a call for him. It was, so we were told, his regular Friday call to Radio Oxford. He said he would take it where he was and he was handed the phone. He told somcone at the other end of the telephone that he was ready.

'Then he said: "Good evening, listeners. No doubt you have heard today how I have taken £50,000 from that scurrilous magazine, *Private Eye*. I am going to give the money to AIDS research."

'Then he added: "And I can tell you this evening that I am going to write a book about my experiences and it is to be called *Malice in Wonderland*."

'So much for secrecy.'

Jackson was also the *Daily Mirror* reporter at the Commonwealth Games in Edinburgh in 1986. These games are now remembered chiefly for two things: the boycott by 32 African nations in protest at Mrs Thatcher's attitude to sanctions against South Africa, and Robert Maxwell's rescue of the Games.

Maxwell was asked to bail the games out when, only eight weeks before the event, the organizers said publicly that unless they could find £5 million the games would not begin. Maxwell agreed to underwrite them and the headline in the *Daily Mirror* was: '*Mirror* Saves the Games.' The headline in the group's sister paper, the Scottish *Daily Record*, was: '*Record* Saves the Games.' Jackson takes up the story:

'Before the start of the games I was covering a lunch in the athletes' village at which Robert Maxwell was due to speak. I received a telephone call from my news editor telling me that Reuter's out of New Delhi were quoting Indian Prime Minister Rajiv Gandhi to the effect that, in view of the African boycott, he was going to delay the departure of the Indian team. I was asked to pass this on to Mr Maxwell. But as I finished my phone call, Mr Maxwell got to his feet and began his speech.

'I thought: "Well, it doesn't really matter because it isn't as if the Indians have decided to join the boycott – they may still be coming."

'Mr Maxwell told his audience that the Games were going to be successful despite the boycott, and that he was pleased to say that the Indian team was on its way. He was challenged from the audience by someone who had heard what the wires were saying from India. Afterwards Maxwell was furious and rang the *Mirror* demanding to know why he hadn't been told. He was informed that the information had been passed on, but that I had evidently failed to give it to him.

'Maxwell rang my boss, Richard Stott, and demanded that I be fired. Stott is said to have replied: "Fire Jackson? But he's the finest centre forward Oxford have ever had." This so nonplussed the great man that no more was said about it.

'Anyway, he was always firing people. The secret was just to ignore it. In most cases he couldn't remember who he'd fired, and if you kept your head down you'd be all right.'

*   *   *

Robert Maxwell was a self-proclaimed royalist but (as John Jackson witnessed) he clearly thought he deserved precedence over everyone else.

'Shortly before the Commonwealth Games began, Maxwell broke his ankle and was hobbling around on crutches. At the opening ceremony he seemed so desperate to get close to the Queen that everyone was convinced that he was going to put his arm around her. In the event what happened was that at the opening ceremony a huge black limousine cruised around the athletic track in front of the royal car. It came to rest by the royal podium. A door swung open and out came this leg in plaster followed by a pair of crutches. As Robert Maxwell emerged the soldiers beside the podium gave him a royal salute.'

To Maxwell the material symbols of his success were useful only if they could be used to enhance his image as a hugely succesful man. His yacht, the *Lady Ghislaine*, and his planes and helicopters were much enjoyed by Maxwell mainly for that reason. But even smaller prizes could be used in that way, as Bob Cole remembers.

'Many years ago I bought him a complete set of *Wisden*, the cricketing almanac. I explained to him that it was a very collectable item. One day as I passed his office I heard him discussing the set with a group of businessmen. He told them how collectable a full set of *Wisden*s was and added: "Even the Queen hasn't got one. She would dearly love one but I have no intention of letting my set go."

'I pointed out to Mr Maxwell that we didn't know if the Queen had a set of *Wisden* or not – or, if she didn't, whether she would really want one.

'He said to me: "I know that, you know that, but they don't know that – and it makes a good story doesn't it?"'

Robert Maxwell liked to think that he was good at everything. He also believed he could recognize an important news item when he saw one. On one occasion he was about to fly out of Heathrow in his private jet when he saw some fire engines and a number of police officers. He knew that the Prime Minister, Mrs Thatcher, was due to leave from Heathrow some time later. So he phoned the newsdesk of the *Daily Mirror* and told them that there was a major security alert at Heathrow and that he expected to see the story on the front page of the *Mirror*. Of course, there are many security alerts at an airport during the course of a day and though precautions have to be taken, very few of these incidents turn out to be newsworthy. So it was with this one.

Unfortunately, Maxwell phoned the newsdesk later to check the progress of the story. When he was told it didn't appear to be as important as was first thought, he was annoyed that someone dared challenge his judgement. So he said he still expected to see the story on the front page. In the end it made a small paragraph on page two. Maxwell was furious.

*   *   *

Ghislaine was Maxwell's favourite child – after all, he named a yacht after her. Maxwell knew that she was a fan of the Rolling Stones and one day he arranged for himself and Ghislaine to have dinner with Mick Jagger. He did it through the pop writer, John Blake, who is a friend of the Rolling Stones' lead singer and who had just joined Mirror Group Newspapers having been recruited from the *Sun*.

Blake and Jagger went up to Maxwell's penthouse apartment to meet the publisher but were kept waiting for half an hour before he turned up. They were let in to wait and, because they were bored, decided to have a look around. They went into Maxwell's bedroom and were amused to find that his huge bed was reinforced with steel underneath.

Eventually Maxwell arrived with Ghislaine and the four went out to dinner. During the evening Maxwell began to boast about how over the years he had made various people stars.

'I can do it to you,' he said pointing at John Blake. 'In a few months' time your name will be up in lights.... There it will be: "Robert Blake".'

*   *   *

Noel Lewis, former Political Correspondent of the *Daily Mirror* remembers his first editorial conference. 'These often took place, as I later found out, on a Sunday. The meeting was just about to start when I heard the sound of a helicopter landing on the top of the roof. I could sense a wave of anxiety flooding the room.

'In came Robert Maxwell and immediately started to chew up some poor chap about a photograph that had appeared

in other papers but not in ours. He demanded to know why
we hadn't got it and told the poor man to go and find out
and to come back immediately. No one sprang to this man's
defence whilst he was being eaten alive, simply because
everyone was glad it wasn't happening to them. As we left
the room I was discussing what had happened with one of
my new colleagues.

'He said: "The trouble is that the Stock Exchange is closed
on a Sunday, so with nothing else to do Maxwell comes
down here and plays with his other f ... ing toy."

'I remember that Robert Maxwell wanted to write a leader
during the Gulf War urging the allies to use a nuclear weapon
against Iraq, but he was persuaded against it.'

*   *   *

Gill Pringle was hired by Mirror Group Newspapers to be
number two to columnist John Blake. On her first day she
was taken up to the boss's offices on the top floor. Maxwell
always liked to meet journalists who'd just been hired. John
Blake was also there to see Gill Pringle sign her contract.

She was very nervous meeting 'The Publisher' for the first
time, but she signed her contract and left the room. To
make polite conversation, John Blake told Maxwell that Gill
Pringle had been married only the week before. Maxwell
relayed a message to call her back. Gill Pringle was told that
Maxwell was calling her back up to his private offices because
he'd found out she was married.

Gill feared the worst – she thought Maxwell might not
approve and that he might fire her. When she arrived back
in the room, he presented her with a cheque for £1,000 as a
wedding present.

*   *   *

As we have seen, Maxwell often couldn't remember who he
had fired and when. Ian Watson was the first editor of *The
European*. Like most of Maxwell's editors he eventually fell
foul of the great man and was sacked. But he became an

Editorial Director of the paper and in October 1991 helped to organize a sumptuous launch for *The European* in America. Six hundred guests were invited to the UN building in New York where a reception was held. David Dinkins, the Mayor of New York, was there as was the UN Secretary General Javier Perez de Cuellar. Ian Watson takes up the story.

'Bob Maxwell kept introducing me to everyone, which annoyed me since I had invited them myself and knew most of them personally. But he kept saying: "I'd like you to meet my editor." I didn't say anything. Next morning we were having breakfast together and he said to me: "Mr Editor, I want you to sack our entire Brussels office." I said: "First of all, Bob, I'm not your editor, you sacked me six months ago, and secondly we have only recently opened our office in Brussels. We have one person working there and they are doing a very good job." He looked at me and said: "Never mind, just get on with it."'

One of *The European*'s executives was due to go to the same launch in New York, but according to Ian Watson, a strange thing happened to him on the way to the reception. 'The executive arrived, as we all tend to do in our profession, at the last minute. As he boarded the plane he was surprised to see an old lady arguing with the cabin staff. It seems she was being told she had to leave. They were telling her she had been recalled to the office. She said that she was on her way to New York to see her grandchildren. But the cabin staff were adamant. She must leave. Of course the message was for our man, R. Lewis – she had the same name and initials and such was Maxwell's power that the cabin staff all but threw her off the plane.'

Sporting Connections

In *Who's Who* Robert Maxwell listed his pastimes as football and chess. His love of football is said to have dated back to the early 1930s when the young 'Maxwell' found out that Arsenal had come to his town. It is said he was so poor that he couldn't watch the game, but managed to get a glimpse of the famous red and white shirts by climbing the walls of the ground.

When Maxwell was in the British Army he played football for his battalion and according to his army pals was a nippy outside left. After that his love for the game lay largely dormant for nearly 40 years as he built a business empire. Then in the 1980s it made a startling reappearance. There are some cynics who suggest that his interest in soccer clubs was more about realizing the property assets of the grounds than about 'the beautiful game'; at all events, he seems to have made a profit on his investments.

Whatever his motives, his first move took place in 1981 when he bought Oxford United. The club was £94,000 in debt, had an overdraft of £164,000, and the bank had lost patience. The club was told they had no more than 10 days left when Maxwell stepped in. Under Maxwell's chairmanship Oxford United rose from the Third to the First Division and they also won the Milk Cup at Wembley in 1986. But along the way Maxwell often clashed with the players, managers, fans and the authorities – especially the Football League management committee, whom he renamed the 'mis-management committee'.

His scheme to merge Oxford and Reading to form Thames Valley FC, which would play at a new ground to be developed at Didcot, was even more unpopular than the sale of Oxford's best player Dean Saunders to Derby County, a club Maxwell had acquired after failing to buy Manchester United.

After Maxwell bought Derby he lost interest in Oxford and installed his son Kevin there as club chairman. Under Maxwell's chairmanship Derby, like Oxford, rose from the Third to the First Division, and Maxwell broadcast regularly on BBC Radio Derby. Then Maxwell again appeared to lose interest. His promises of money to buy new players never materialized, though he was often in the news over plans to buy Watford from Elton John or to help bail Tottenham Hotspur out of financial difficulties.

In the 1989–90 season Maxwell spent a total of less than one hour watching Derby play at the Baseball Ground. On one occasion he flew in by helicopter to watch the team play an important cup tie against Arsenal but left before half time in order to go on a mercy mission abroad. As he left, the fans chanted: 'He's fat, he's round, he's never at the ground, Captain Bob, Captain Bob!'

Derby's supporters turned against him because they believed he'd starved the club of the funds it needed to win the First Division title. This turning tide of opinion was, of course, reflected on Radio Derby, and Maxwell took exception to it. He was particularly annoyed when in a phone-in programme the presenter suggested fans should jam Maxwell's switchboard with protest calls. Maxwell threatened legal action and had the presenter banned from the ground.

Shortly afterwards Maxwell decided to sell Derby and in August 1990 he embroiled himself in the affairs of another club, Tottenham Hotspur. Spurs were facing mounting debts and their club chairman, Irving Scholar, was worried he would have to sell two of his world cup stars, Paul Gascoigne and Gary Lineker (Spurs still owed Barcelona £850,000, which was outstanding on Lineker's transfer fee). Once again Maxwell was asked to be the saviour.

The idea was that he would underwrite a £12 million rights issue and pay off the outstanding fee to Barcelona through one of his private companies, Headington Investments. As far as Maxwell was concerned it would put him in the driving seat of one of Europe's best-known clubs. But there was one major obstacle to overcome: the Football League would never agree to his owning two First Division clubs, Derby County and Spurs. So he announced that all his football interests were up for sale – though, of course, he had a secret agreement with Scholar. Eventually this came out when a report by a City law firm criticized the Spurs chairman for agreeing a secret deal and the Stock Exchange suspended dealings in Spurs' shares. Scholar was forced to resign. Eventually Spurs' manager Terry Venables and Alan Sugar, founder of the computer firm Amstrad, stepped in, and over Maxwell, to take over the club.

Maxwell's involvement in football exhibits all the characteristics which can be seen in the other compartments of his life. There were many inter-club deals, and there are suggestions that Maxwell put the money from transfer fees straight into his own pocket and not into the club bank accounts. He moved from one club to another, always convinced in his own mind that he was the only one who could save that particular club and that it was only because they wouldn't listen to him that things went wrong.

His football deals suffered from the same problems as his business ones. He would tire very easily of his new toy, and then see a much nicer one in the shop window. He would become obsessed with owning it, but since the sport's ruling bodies took a strict view about the number of clubs one man could own, he would inevitably fall foul of the authorities. There would then be a period of recrimination and eventually Maxwell would storm out, claiming the problems had been caused by everyone except himself. In the end, though, I suspect that one of the reasons his football deals went wrong in the later years is that he simply didn't have the spare money to play around with.

Sports writer Frank Keating feels a little guilty because he thinks he may have contributed towards the creation of Maxwell the monster – the beast that tried to devour football clubs.

'I was introduced to Robert Maxwell by his daughter Christine. I'd met her in Los Angeles, where she was working. At home in England she suddenly called me up and invited me to dinner at Headington Hill Hall. She said her father was anxious to meet me. I had been told he had been a goalkeeper in the past but at this time he had no involvement in football. I thought he might want to talk to me about writing a school book about football.

'He was particularly affable. The four or five other guests present were eastern European boffins. Half way through the meal Maxwell announced that he had to go and sort out a dispute at the *Radio Times*. But first he spoke to me about a review I had written for the *Guardian* about Desmond Morris's book *The Soccer Tribe*. It knocked the idea that soccer hooligans took after the apes. Maxwell seemed delighted when I tore Morris's argument to shreds.

'I stayed the night and the next morning I said goodbye to Christine and Ghislaine, who drove me to the station. Both girls seemed grateful that I had given Dad the low down on football. Three weeks later Maxwell took over Oxford United and it was only then that I realized that Desmond Morris was a director of the club. So in a way I blame myself for introducing Maxwell to football.'

Keating may blame himself for creating the monster but, as far as professional man-watcher, author and broadcaster Desmond Morris is concerned, Maxwell was wonderful subject-matter:

'When Robert Maxwell took over as Chairman of Oxford United Football Club I suddenly found myself in an ideal position to do some Maxwell-watching. For a student of body language like myself he was a feast and I was fascinated by the way in which he cultivated the unexpected as a way of making himself the centre of attention.

'His strategy was NOT to behave in precisely the way everyone anticipated he would behave in a given social context. He was sometimes more formal than expected, sometimes less formal; sometimes orthodox, sometimes eccentric. And it was impossible to guess which it would be at any particular time. This created an edginess in those around him that worked in his favour. It also made him the subject of endless anecdotes (as this book proves), which all helped him to create the Maxwell myth.

'It also helped him to hide the moments when he really did not know how to deal with a matter of social etiquette. Such lapses could be put down as just another of his deliberate eccentricities. On the day he bought the football club, for instance, he insisted on meeting the players on the pitch. Arriving at the ground he despatched an aide to the club shop to find an Oxford United rosette, pinned it to his overcoat and strode out onto the turf to shake hands with everyone. No other football club chairman would dream of wearing a rosette in that way. Rosettes have hardly been used by adult fans since the 1940s, except perhaps by fanatical supporters on the way to Wembley on Cup Final day. Maxwell was confusing his days on the hustings as a Labour politician – when a rosette would have been appropriate – with the modern football context in which he found himself. To his players it suggested that he hadn't been to a football match since he was a young man; which was probably true.

'I used my brief contact with Maxwell to carry out one or two simple experiments. For example, there was the moment of the annual team photograph. This essential little football ritual involved all the directors of the club turning up in their dark suits and sitting in seats surrounded by the whole playing squad, all in their new strip for the coming season. A large copy of this formalized scene would then be hung on the boardroom wall, alongside all those taken on previous years. No director ever dared miss the ritual occasion.

'Maxwell duly arrived and sat in the centre of the ground. The photographer fussed with his lenses and announced that he was ready. At this point Maxwell stood up, took off his dark suit jacket, shoved it under his chair and sat down again. The photograph was taken and we all dispersed, Maxwell quickly putting on his jacket again and striding off. When the picture appeared on the boardroom wall, there in the very centre of the group was a large white blob. Maxwell's shirt had made him the conspicuous and highly contrasting centre-piece of the composition. The formality of the dark suits of the other directors set them apart from him, like flunkies. His trivial action had succeeded in making him "special".

'I was amazed that he would have been so sensitive to such a tiny gain in the game of one-upmanship. When the time for the next annual team photo arrived I decided to try a little test. Instead of wearing the obligatory dark suit, I put on a light-weight, white summer jacket. This, I reasoned, would create a dilemma for Maxwell. If he slipped off his jacket he would no longer be a uniquely white blob in the centre of the photograph. So what would he do to make himself special? Perhaps my action would force him to order up a funny hat from the club shop? We gathered on the pitch and I waited with amusement to observe the Maxwell ploy.

'I should have known better. He simply failed to turn up at all. The final score: Maxwell 1, Morris nil.'

Peter Marsh was also a director of Oxford United and had been brought in as a friend of Desmond Morris. But within 10 days it was apparent that he and Maxwell simply couldn't work together. He resigned when Maxwell refused to honour a managerial contract which had been drawn up and signed by the previous club chairman.

'It was still sitting in the Chairman's in-tray so I gave a copy to the man concerned so that if Maxwell didn't honour it he would have something to show that he had been offered such a contract. I then resigned. Normally when a director resigns a statement is issued to the press saying he's gone "for personal or business reasons". In this case no such statement was prepared. Maxwell seemed to believe that if you had resigned, he'd dismissed you.

'At the time, I was a humble polytechnic lecturer but Maxwell was always boasting about the million pound deals he was doing. I thought it was strange for him to want to boast to the likes of me. I was always suspicious of him and, though I don't like to say "told you so", I did tell the other members of the board. Eventually, of course, relations between Maxwell and the club did sour, especially over the ridiculous scheme to merge Reading and Oxford United football clubs. I was vehemently opposed to it, as were both sets of fans. But I remember Maxwell saying: "Only the Thames running backwards will stop this deal going forwards."

'We did manage to stop it, though. Maxwell didn't seem to understand the fans or the football rules which would prevent it. He believed he could just do whatever he wanted. I mean, you had to dislike a man who walked into a club board meeting with a cigar in his mouth, barked "Light!", and expected someone to rush up with some matches or a lighter.'

Mark Lawrenson, the great Liverpool and Ireland central defender, became manager of Oxford United after Robert Maxwell left to become Chairman of Derby County Football Club. Lawrenson's chairman was Kevin Maxwell.

'I'd taken over the manager's job at Oxford United with about 10 days to go before the end of the season. We were desperately trying to fend off relegation.

'One Saturday we were playing Southampton. At half time I was trying to rally the troops during the team talk in the dressing room. There are two entrances and I had my back to one of them. I sensed that someone had come in judging by the expressions on the lads' faces. I turned round to see Robert Maxwell sitting on a bench wearing his Derby County baseball cap.

'He said: "It's all right, just carry on."'

Maxwell was said to be a heavy gambler and there are stories that he lost very heavily in the London casinos in the weeks before he died. Some say he could lose a quarter of a million pounds a night. But he was also quite capable of winning.

In the season that Oxford United gained promotion to the Second Division, Maxwell placed an £18,000 bet on them to win the Second Division championship. He also placed a smaller bet on them winning promotion. At the end of the football season Maxwell showed his winnings to Joe Haines – a cheque for £223,000. Haines asked him what he was going to do with it.

Maxwell replied: 'I don't know, I'll probably give it to the club.' He appeared completely indifferent about the money. What had excited him was backing his hunch and winning.

There was one man on the *Daily Mirror* who was a notorious toady. One day two of the reporters walked past him, chatting as they went. One of them said to the other what good news it was that Derby County had won their cup tie. The second asked the score and was told it was four goals to nil. They then sat some way away from the sycophant and awaited developments. Almost immediately he picked up the phone to pass on his congratulations to Maxwell. There followed a brief exchange which the two journalists monitored with amusement. The sycophant kept saying: 'Oh! Oh! Oh!' and then put the phone down. Derby County hadn't been playing that day.

Mark Lawrenson recalls an incident that sheds light on Kevin Maxwell's position as Chairman of Oxford United. 'In August 1988 or '89, I was trying to buy a left back: 23-year-old Jimmy Phillips, who'd played for Doncaster Rovers but was now at Glasgow Rangers. He was surplus to their requirements but was a good player.

'I went up to Glasgow with my assistant, Brian Horton (who's now manager of Oxford United). We'd seen Phillips play and so we wanted to see the Rangers manager Graeme

Souness on the night before Rangers' first league game of the season. After some negotiation we agreed a fee of £150,000.

'I said that should be fine but I had to phone my Chairman, Kevin Maxwell, to OK the fee. He was away for the weekend on board the *Lady Ghislaine* but had given me a telephone number. I finally got through to the yacht after what seemed an eternity and a big, booming voice answered: it was Robert Maxwell.

'I said: "Hello, Mr Maxwell, it's Mark Lawrenson. Can I speak to Kevin about a player we want to sign from Glasgow Rangers?"

'"Speak," said the voice.

'I explained that I needed Kevin's approval.

'Again the voice simply said: "Speak."

'I told him who the player was and Robert Maxwell asked how much Rangers wanted.

'"A hundred and fifty thousand pounds," I replied.

'"How old is he?" asked Maxwell. I told him the player was 23.

'"Consider it done," said the voice, and put the phone down.

'Robert Maxwell, the chairman of a rival football club – Derby County – had just authorized spending a large sum of Oxford United's money. I found it quite incredible.'

Lionel Pickering, now the majority shareholder in Derby County FC, found dealing with Maxwell very difficult indeed. 'It was a year ago last September when Maxwell was trying to buy Tottenham Hotspur. I put in a £3 million bid to buy the club he currently owned, Derby County. I heard nothing and in January of the next year I thought my scheme was a dead duck. So I told BBC Radio Derby that four months before I had offered £3 million to buy Derby County but had never even had a response from Robert Maxwell.

'The sports commentator, Graham Ritchie, knew that the fans would be outraged at this news and in a radio phone-in programme encouraged them to telephone Maxwell and

jam his switchboard in protest, which many of them did.
Maxwell was incensed by this and decided to ban Ritchie
and myself from Derby's football ground. Amusingly, in one
of the match programmes he described me as: "an unfit
person to do business with". I believe it was the greatest
compliment he ever paid anyone!

'Maxwell claimed my offer was far too low and that the
club was worth £8 million. He'd paid less than half a million
for it in 1984! So, in the end, rather than sell to me, he sold
the club to a consortium of local businessmen. They paid
him nearly £4 million, which was ridiculous because Derby
were about to be relegated to the Second Division and
Maxwell had already agreed to sell the club's two best
players, Wright and Saunders, to Liverpool.

'The money for those two players should have gone to the
club. It is against Football League rules for club chairmen
to receive a penny of transfer fees. Needless to say Maxwell
got his hands on the money, so when he departed he left the
club £2 million in debt. We also discovered that nearly
£800,000 was owed by Derby County to Oxford United,
another Maxwell club.

'Though the consortium paid over the odds for the club,
the members felt – as did the rest of the city – that Maxwell
had to go at any cost. People in Derby felt let down by him.
He'd promised the fans that the club would win the First
Division Championship and would once more be competing
for honours in Europe. In their first season back in Division
One they finished fifth and the manager, Arthur Cox, told
me that if they could have bought one or two players they
would have had a serious crack at the First Division title
the following season. But Maxwell suddenly lost interest in
the club and wouldn't allow the manager to spend anything
on transfers over the next two years. People wouldn't have
felt so bad if he'd not promised them great things or if he'd
been honest with them.

'When Maxwell sold to the consortium he insisted that
Graham Ritchie, the Radio Derby sports commentator,

should continue to be banned from the ground for five years after the sale. When the consortium found out just how bad the financial situation was the members came to me. As a result, I now own 78 per cent of the shares.

'We have tried to get around the Graham Ritchie ban; he is allowed into the ground, but as yet is not allowed to go into the press box. Maxwell's influence lives on even after his death.'

Gary Richardson, now a BBC Radio sports reporter, remembers an episode from Maxwell's Oxford United days. 'I went to Oxford United to interview Robert Maxwell on what was supposed to be the greatest moment in the club's history – on the day they won promotion from the Second to the First Division.

'Mr Maxwell said it would be better to do the interview in the back of his car, where it would be less noisy. We settled into the back of the Rolls Royce and as I turned my tape recorder on Maxwell looked at his chauffeur and said: "Drive". The car began moving slowly out of the ground. I didn't think he would go far, so I kept my tape recorder going. We pulled on to the main road. Robert Maxwell wouldn't talk about Oxford's promotion to Division One, all he wanted to talk about was Oxford City Council. He kept on saying they'd lied and cheated and that they'd gone back on a promise to give the club a new ground. Still the car kept going. I thought we would end up on the ring road.

'Eventually I rather meekly said to Maxwell that I hoped he wasn't going too far because I had to get back with my report. He said he was going on to his home but then the driver would take me wherever I wanted. So we went to Headington Hill Hall, and then the driver took me back to the ground.'

*   *   *

When Robert Maxwell 'saved' the Commonwealth Games, Hewden Stuart, a plant hire company based in Glasgow had already supplied goods and services valued at more than

£47,000 to the games. The company's chairman, Mathew Goodwin, now Sir Mathew Goodwin, says that the company hadn't received any payment. Then he received a letter from Bob Maxwell.

'It told me there weren't sufficient funds and that he, Maxwell, proposed to pay off all the small creditors, i.e. up to £5,000, and that the larger creditors would surrender half of their claim with the balance being paid in instalments. I took the view that this was grossly unfair. The smaller creditors might turn out to be multinational companies like British Petroleum, while the larger creditors would undoubtedly include many small local firms who had supplied the games. Accordingly I instructed my solicitors to advise Maxwell that unless the letter was withdrawn forthwith I would apply to the Scottish Courts for an Inhibition against Maxwell proceeding in this way, thus running the risk that no one would be paid. A few days later I arrived at my office to be told that Mr Maxwell had phoned and left a telephone number. I dialled and the phone at the other end was picked up by Mr Maxwell himself, despite the fact that he had all the problems of the games, that he was involved in a major libel action and a couple of takeover bids. Maxwell was charm itself. When I made it clear I was prepared to proceed with litigation, Maxwell told me that my account would be paid in full. He then proceeded to question me about my business, my family, my view of the games, industry and even the weather. He seemed to have all the time in the world and was on the phone for nearly an hour. He even suggested that we met for lunch – of course, we never did. A few days later I received a cheque and the account was paid in full. But I later found out that other people hadn't been paid. I think Maxwell paid me rather than go to court because he believed if he paid me and kept it quiet then many of the other creditors would simply accept his assurance that the money was lost and wouldn't press to be paid.

The Inner Circle

Robert Maxwell treated his executives like servants, and his servants like executives. His 'inner circle' of chauffeurs, chefs, and butlers were often dealt with more civilly than his closest 'advisers'. Of course, one of the problems was that Maxwell often refused to heed advice. He liked to be pampered, he liked people to fuss over him, and in a strange way he liked servants to stand up for themselves against him. If they did they were respected and treated very well.

Maxwell's servants were paid higher wages than they could ever have found elsewhere. This was often one of the tactics which Maxwell used in order to secure loyalty. Then there were the perks; most of his domestic staff were given company cars with telephones, and could charge petrol and phone bills to expenses. Many of them travelled with Maxwell wherever he went. One valet visited some 40 countries in Maxwell's employment.

Apart from the obvious inducements, Maxwell added a special ingredient: the feeling of being part of an extended family. He would share the kitchen with a chef and try and teach him how to cook. He would insist that his personal servants were treated as well as he was. On the yacht, the *Lady Ghislaine*, his staff had suites, not small guest rooms. If they had personal problems he would sort them out; if they were ill he would often pay for treatment. One secretary, who was with Maxwell for eight years in the 1950s, was told by her doctor that she had to live at a high altitude for six months; so she went to India and Maxwell paid for everything. One of his personal servants developed an ear infection while on board the *Lady Ghislaine*. Despite the fact that the yacht was sailing off the Sardinian coast, Maxwell ordered a boat to be lowered and the man was taken ashore for immediate medical attention; again, Maxwell paid for everything.

'If you had a problem you could always speak to him about it, he wasn't unapproachable,' said one of his inner circle. 'This isn't to say that he didn't ever tell any of his personal servants off – he did. But if he were in the wrong he would often make it up to them.'

Maxwell could relax in the company of the inner circle in a way he could not with anyone else. He would sometimes get drunk with them, especially when they were abroad, when there would be lavish entertainment aboard the *Lady Ghislaine*. He would conspire with his inner circle against people he saw as pompous. For example, he might say something outrageous to someone at a party he was hosting, winking at one of his butlers as he did so.

It's from his inner circle that we get some idea of his more individual quirks and foibles. Who would believe that Maxwell was a fanatical Clint Eastwood fan, who once went into a video shop in New York and bought copies of every Eastwood film.

Towards the end of his life, several of his executives have said, he would rarely eat out for fear of being poisoned. Wherever he went he would take his personal chef and a butler. Maxwell's daily routine was often made up as he went along, but he always began the day at about 6 am, when he would be served coffee and orange juice. He would often have fresh soup for lunch and his main meal of the day would be in the evening, when he would have a starter followed by a choice of three or four main courses. He was particularly fond of fish, especially fresh salmon, smoked salmon, turbot and halibut. He liked free-range chicken and lobster. He liked soups, asparagus, matzos (unleavened bread) and gherkins. He disliked creamy sauces, and described turnips as 'food for pigs'. He even tried his hand at cooking himself, once producing clouds of smoke in an attempt to show his chef Martin Cheeseman how to prepare potato latkes.

As Sir Bernard Audley recalls, 'He had a marvellous taste in caviar, which he would always preface with the words: "Mikhail Gorbachev has sent me this." It was probably true. So you could always guarantee, when you went up to the tenth floor – the holy of holies – an ample supply of caviar.

'His butler, Joseph, supervised the wine cellar; he had only the finest wines, and his taste in wines was impeccable. But *was* it his taste – anymore than the decor of the penthouse which was interior designed for him? Probably not.'

Those who knew Maxwell, but were not so protectively loyal as his inner circle say he never seemed to stop eating. He always had food in his office, particularly in the late afternoon when his butler would bring in trays full of goodies. There would be cheese on toast and bowls of peanuts and crisps. Sometimes champagne was on offer.

Maxwell's appetite for food was perhaps matched only by his appetite for litigation, and he always had a small army of solicitors acting for him at any one time. One of these vividly recalls Maxwell abusing those around him, but insists he was very generous when it came to hospitality – a generosity attested by the fact that one West End solicitor put on a stone in weight during the three years he worked on Maxwell's libel cases.

'Going up to Bob's offices was like going to a wedding feast.' I wanted to ask where the bride and groom were. There was always a long table full of food: toasted cheese, smoked salmon, buckets of caviar, and brown bread. The executives always dined well: good food and fine wines. I remember at coffee time Robert Maxwell had his own cup, on which was printed "I am a very important person." It resembled a soup bowl and Maxwell had to use two hands to drink out of it. Often small snacks would arrive in the middle of meetings and were handed out by his butler Joseph from a large silver tray. We would all take one and the tray would then be passed to Maxwell who would finish off the rest. He was almost always eating, particularly in the afternoons around five or six o'clock.'

*   *   *

Maxwell was very particular about certain items of shopping. He used to insist on Marks and Spencer's peanuts and crisps, and would only use red toothbrushes. And though he was very fond of pickled gherkins, only one particular brand would do.

Bob Cole was often called upon to buy these sort of items at shops near his Bromley home. On one occasion, however, he had to look farther afield.

'Maxwell had heard that there had been a disastrous failure of the cucumber crop in Poland and Hungary and that as a consequence pickled cucumbers would be in short supply. He had me and a number of others going around Hendon and Golders Green buying up all the jars we could lay hands on. Of course, there proved to be no truth in the crop-failure rumour, but for months and months afterwards the refreshment table at any function held at Mirror Group headquarters in High Holborn had to have large quantities of sliced pickled cucumber so we could get rid of the gherkins we'd bought.'

Maxwell liked to be pampered, to be the centre of attention whatever the cost, because he needed to appear the rich, powerful tycoon, and his personal servants were as much part of that image as his helicopter and his yacht. But they were even more important because many of them knew a lot about Maxwell – they knew his secrets. In exchange for their high salaries and fair treatment, they fussed over him and gave him the loyalty he couldn't buy elsewhere. When he landed on the roof of Maxwell House in the helicopter he would be brought a cup of tea. In winter when he suffered from the colds to which he was prone (he had only one lung), he expected those in the inner circle to know about it and to make a fuss of him. On one occasion, when his chauffeur carried a coat and scarf into a hotel where he was dining, Maxwell protested to his fellow guests: 'They'll run your life if you let them.' But he loved being pampered.

It is perhaps not so strange that the people Maxwell seemed most at ease with were the voters in Buckingham and his personal servants. I suppose he still liked to feel himself a man of the people who had never totally left behind his Czech peasant roots. After all, he delighted in picking up his soup bowl and dispensing with the spoon – even at the poshest functions. He insisted that he lived in the 'grandest council house in England' (he rented Headington Hill Hall from Oxford City Council). And his curious conviction that he was a socialist persisted to the end. In his relations with his inner circle he displayed the qualities which made him a good constituency MP and a fine soldier.

John Featley, who was Maxwell's chauffeur from March 1988 until the tycoon's death, remembers one day when several of the staff were helping Maxwell pack his personal belongings for a trip to America. While they were sorting out which of his briefcases he should take, they opened one and found that it contained $800,000 in cash. Maxwell simply told them to take it out and put it in the safe.

Maxwell wasn't lavish when it came to spending on his own car. It was a B-registered (1984) Rolls Royce and Featley says he was always trying to persuade Maxwell to get rid of it as it seemed to spend most of its time in the garage being repaired. It was fitted out in a pretty standard way, but it had two phones in it at all times: a master phone, which could not be taken out of the car, and a hand portable in a cradle at the back. Maxwell always carried a third phone in his pocket. There was sometimes a mobile fax machine as well, which could be plugged into the cigarette lighter.

Whatever Maxwell did and wherever he went, he was always late, according to John Featley. 'One day we were running late as usual, but I had looked in the diary and saw that we were due to go to the Spanish embassy for drinks and then on to meet Mrs Maxwell at Sotheby's in New Bond Street. Eventually he came down from his office, opened the car door and sat in the back of the Rolls Royce. I set off for the embassy.

'Suddenly Mr Maxwell shouted: "Where the f... are we going?"

'"To the Spanish embassy," I replied.

'He went mad. He told me he didn't have enough time to go for drinks before meeting Mrs Maxwell. He tore me off a strip and blamed me for not asking. I was angry. I pulled the car over and said I didn't know why he was so worried about Mrs Maxwell, it had never bothered him before.

'"How was I supposed to know the timetable had changed if no one told me?" I asked. Everything in the back of the car suddenly fell silent and I thought to myself: "John, you've done it now! You've lost your job."

'Then Mr Maxwell calmly said to me: "John, next time we are running late and we have a number of appointments, just turn round and ask me which ones we should go to." And that was it. I found if you stood up to him he treated you with a little more respect.'

When Maxwell went to America he would take his own valet, butler and chef with him as well as his own personal secretary. But on some occasions that wasn't possible. If any of them were on holiday, he would look for replacements locally. As a result there are a number of men in the United States who have worked for Maxwell for short periods as butlers. One of them is James Tissot, whose regular job was as the maître d' for Macmillan Inc. When Maxwell knew that James was to double as his butler he sent him a seven-page fax detailing his culinary likes and dislikes.

Tissot can't remember exactly what was on the list, but he says: 'Maxwell liked a wide range of food from pleasant, cheap food, like beans on toast, to expensive caviar. I remember two items that were never served when he was there: garlic and onions. He liked very fine wines and when he was around we budgeted a staggering $4,000 an afternoon on stock.

'My first encounter with him was in Philadelphia. He came over and we travelled to Philadelphia with him from New York. He took both of his private jets. Kevin Maxwell's secretary was acting as his secretary, and Mr and Mrs Maxwell were both going to Temple University to receive honorary degrees for their work on the Holocaust.

'We stayed in three different hotels in three days. It was at the time when the Ayatollah Khomeini had declared a *fatwah* on the author Salman Rushdie for his book *The Satanic Verses*. What I didn't know until later was that Mr Maxwell had said that if Salman Rushdie was murdered he would pay a $5 million reward to anyone who brought the killer to justice. Apparently, this gesture made him a terrorist target, too. We were met at the airport by four big black limousines, two of which were empty and were there only as terrorist decoys. We had the Secret Service with us, and retrieving the luggage from the airport turned into a major headache. One of the cars had to go back from the Four Seasons Hotel to pick up the bags. In general the trip was a nightmare and during it I felt like resigning. Mr Maxwell was very difficult. But I kept at it and after I'd stood up for myself on a couple of occasions, life with him got a lot better.

'Money really was no object. He spent $2,000 hiring a suite of rooms so that I could lay out lunch and cocktails. We had a full bar. There were a few guests but the whole lunch had to last no longer than 45 minutes because Mr Maxwell had to go on to a meeting. So $2,000 for a room for 45 minutes seems a lot of money.

'Then there was the plane. Mr and Mrs Maxwell flew back to Britain in the larger of the two private planes. The secretary and I flew to New York in the smaller one. We were the only passengers. We would have been just as happy going by train.'

*   *   *

Maxwell could be charming when he wanted to – but he could destroy people with a few poisoned barbs as well. He often reduced even his executives to tears. One story illustrates both aspects of his character at once.

He had been shouting all day at everyone near him. One of his secretaries in particular had come in for a tongue lashing – she'd been called all the names under the sun by her boss. Towards the end of the working day Maxwell was again nasty to her and a short time later she burst into tears. When Maxwell emerged from his office he saw her crying at her desk.

Maxwell rushed over and demanded: 'Who did this to you? I'll sack him!'

*   *   *

In 1988 one of Maxwell's inner circle was due to go away on a rugby tour. He had warned his boss well in advance, but Maxwell – who believed employees should be available seven days a week, 52 weeks a year – wasn't keen on losing his services even for a short while. In the weeks leading up to the tour Maxwell was particularly difficult and the relationship between them became strained. The employee was due to depart at the weekend, so on the Friday before he reminded Mr Maxwell about his trip and said that there were a number of matters that had to be dealt with before he left.

Maxwell expressed the view that the rugby tour was 'just a piss up'. His employee agreed but said it was no less enjoyable for that and he still intended to go. He pressed Maxwell about the matters he wanted to clear up before he went. Maxwell replied that he had no time to deal with them.

The employee said he had to depart at one o'clock the next day but was willing to come in on Saturday morning in order to tie up the loose ends. Maxwell finally agreed and said that the man should be there at eight the following morning.

At eight o'clock on Saturday morning the employee was at the office, waiting to see Maxwell. He was still waiting at

11.45 am. When he was finally let into the presence, Maxwell was still reluctant to consider any of the points his employee wanted to clear up. Finally he said: 'All right then, Mister, pick your best three.'

Three items of business were duly put before Maxwell, who agreed and signed all of them without even reading what they were about. The employee was annoyed with Maxwell's behaviour, but relieved that he could finally get away on his rugby tour. Maxwell's son, Kevin, was in the room and the employee realized that with Maxwell one person amounted to an audience, so he was probably playing to the gallery.

As he walked to the door to leave, Maxwell called him back. He feared the worst.

'Just a minute!' said Maxwell. 'If you're going on this piss up I suppose you'll need some beer money.' He pulled out of his pocket £1,000 in cash and handed it over to the bewildered man.

* * *

If ever there was a man born to sit on the back seat of a Rolls Royce then I suppose he would end up looking pretty much like Robert Maxwell. Apart from anything else he was just the right size to benefit from such a car. But as everyone knows, a Rolls Royce is more than a vehicle – it's a statement. It's part of the image for the rich and famous.

Maxwell was always concerned about his image. In the last months of his life his empire survived on little more than the hope that Captain Bob would be able to keep the various plates spinning. People are naturally inclined to have confidence in those who have confidence in themselves. The Rolls Royce, the private yacht, the helicopter, being on friendly terms with the world's leaders were all important contributing factors to the continued survival of the Maxwell empire. And incidents like the following must have kept confidence amongst Maxwell's creditors fairly high and stopped them calling in their debts.

A former employee says that Maxwell was driving in his Rolls Royce along the Strand on the way to a dinner at the Savoy Hotel. He was reading a hand-written note. The employee says that Maxwell showed it to him, and though he can't recall exactly what it said he remembers that it began 'Dear Bob' and was signed 'George'. It was from the President of the United States and appeared to be thanking Maxwell for the advice he'd given Bush about the changes in Russia and Eastern Europe. As Maxwell read the letter the car phone rang. President Mitterrand of France was on the line, also wanting to discuss the implications of the downfall of communism.

Incidents like this were vitally important to Maxwell; they boosted his ego but, more importantly, added to his image as a world statesman-without-portfolio. It encouraged others to have confidence in him; ultimately, I suppose, it indirectly boosted the share price of his companies and kept them afloat that much longer.

*   *   *

Maxwell was self obsessed. So even during the negotiations with the unions over Maxwell's plan to buy the New York *Daily News*, Maxwell came first for Maxwell. James Tissot says his employer would often take a nap in the afternoon. Maxwell told him that his attitude was that anyone who wanted to see him could either wait until he woke up, or go away.

Maxwell would often test people who worked for him by being as obnoxious as possible and seeing if they would break. Either they became completely subservient and did exactly what he wanted all the time, or they would stand up for themselves and gain a little respect. James Tissot said that at some point in 1988 or 1989 Maxwell was trying out another local butler. The new man phoned Tissot for some advice about buying wine, and Tissot took the opportunity of asking him how it was going.

'Maxwell was a closet eater and a messy one. He would

spit watermelon seeds all over the floor; orange peel and bananas were left lying around for the butler to pick up. I asked how things were going and the new butler said: "It's terrible." He told me he had decided to resign. Then he complained that at the moment Maxwell was eating ribs. He told me that when Maxwell had finished with each one he threw it on the floor and would expect the butler to pick it up.'

* * *

Robert Maxwell was absent-minded about his personal appearance. It was said that secretaries used to whistle as a signal to Maxwell that his trouser zips were undone. One lawyer of his used to sing: '... dip, dip, do ...', and Maxwell would then reach down and zip up.

* * *

Maxwell wasn't noted as a joke teller and it's easy to see why. On one occasion he was at a loose end and came out of his office to mooch about. One of his secretaries asked if she could tell him a joke.

'Of course you can,' he replied.

The secretary asked: 'Mr Maxwell, what did the elephant say to the naked man?' In the time-honoured way Maxwell responded by saying: 'I don't know, tell me, what did the elephant say to the naked man?'

The secretary said: 'The elephant said, how do you manage to eat with one of those?'

Maxwell roared with laughter and then walked off back to his office. As he approached the door he stopped, turned round and asked: 'But why should the elephant say that?'

Everyone else present had to contain their laughter for fear he would think it was at his expense. But it was obvious he didn't understand the punchline.

* * *

Maxwell's policy was that those who worked for him did so

in whatever capacity he required. Even senior executives were
expected to pick up his laundry if it needed to be picked up,
or to fetch him his suit if he needed a change of clothing.
However, this 'larger than life' character never did things by
halves. Bob Cole remembers one request in particular.

'It was about 10.15pm on Friday night in London when
I received a call from Mr Maxwell. It was a busy time. He'd
only just signed the deal to take over the New York *Daily
News*. He phoned to ask if I could get him his dinner suit
and his row of medals. He said I knew where they were and
that he had to go to a dinner.

'I said: "It should be no problem. When is the dinner?"

'He said it was the following evening. It was the "Gridiron"
dinner at the Capitol Hilton in Washington. The Gridiron
is the dinner hosted by America's top satirists and the guest
list included the President of the United States, senators,
bankers, judges – in fact everyone who is anyone in America.

'I agreed to bring the suit, but when I made inquiries I
realized that the only way I could get it to him in time was
to fly Concorde, so that is what I did. I set off early on
Saturday morning and I arrived in Washington around three
o'clock in the afternoon. I went to his hotel and used the
buzzer to ring up to his room. Through the intercom I said:
"It's Bob Cole."

'A voice I recognized replied: "I know that, you fool,
come up!"

'I went up to the room, where Mr Maxwell was being
interviewed by two reporters from *Playboy*. I thought I might
have a hard time explaining the cost of the Concorde flight,
but Mr Maxwell turned to me and said more to the reporters
than to myself: "Here is my only true friend because only a
true friend would drop everything and fly all this way because
I needed something for dinner tonight."

'Naturally, the story of my travelling to America on
Concorde simply to deliver Bob Maxwell's dinner suit made
headlines in the US papers. But Mr Maxwell was overjoyed.
It was obviously a great image for him – the incredibly

wealthy businessman who could even afford to pay for a Concorde ticket for his dinner suit.'

* * *

According to John Featley, Maxwell was most concerned about how he arrived anywhere. He wanted to do it in style, to be noticed – so it would be the Rolls Royce, with the chauffeur opening the door. But when he left a dinner or whatever it was he was attending, Maxwell would quite often take a cab home.

Still, he could be particular about individual arrangements. Every year he went to the World Economic Forum in Davos, Switzerland. Two days before the event began, his chauffeur John Featley, would take the Range Rover and drive down to Davos. Maxwell would fly to Zurich and then take a helicopter to Davos, where the Range Rover would meet him from the helicopter and take him to his hotel.

Featley says he would spend up to four days there and then take Maxwell to catch the return helicopter and onward flight to London. Featley would then drive all the way back to England. In total, he would be away from home for 10 days and drive 1,762 miles simply to take Maxwell from the helicopter to his Swiss hotel and back again.

* * *

As must be obvious by now, Maxwell liked 'collecting' famous people. In both Britain and the United States he had a number of former senior political figures working for him. In 1986 he hired Peter Jay, a former British Ambassador to Washington. Jay was to be a White-House style 'chief of staff'. Maxwell treated Jay like he treated all his business staff – badly. Jay's job, by his own admission, was to try and bring some order to the chaos surrounding Maxwell's business methods. Jay later said that, by his own standards, he failed to do so.

Inside the organization Jay was sometimes known as 'the car park attendant' because he once wrote a memo about reserving parking space for Maxwell's Rolls Royce. But if you worked for Maxwell, no matter what your job title, you did what Maxwell told you to do. Jay later acknowledged this: 'I had no complaints. Nothing was outside what I expected or regarded as legitimate, once I'd agreed to take his money.'

In late 1989, after more than three years with Maxwell, Jay was dismissed. Since then he has refused to criticize Maxwell in public. In a telephone conversation 18 months after his sacking, Jay offered Maxwell some advice on a cold the publisher was having difficulty getting rid of.

Maxwell suddenly exclaimed: 'You're the only friend I have.'

Jay responded by saying: 'Bob, don't be ridiculous.'

He describes his continuing loyalty to Maxwell thus: 'Old-fashioned English schoolboy that I am, if you take someone's cheque, it is not civilized or respectable, the moment you're out of the door, to bad-mouth the guy. I didn't and I suppose that explains why he called me his only friend. I was in no sense his friend.'

When I spoke to Peter Jay I asked him if he could give me one anecdote which summed up, in some way, Maxwell's character.

'One characteristic of the man was courage. Some may say crazy courage, courage both physical and mental. It was best illustrated when he won the Military Cross. But there was one occasion when I was present which showed both his recklessness and his courage. It took place in Kenya in about 1987, or it may have been half a year before or after, and concerns an encounter with a rhinoceros!

'We were in Nairobi at the invitation of the Kenyan President, Daniel Arap Moi. Mr Maxwell was giving them advice on how to relaunch the newspaper of the ruling party, the *Kenya Times*. While we were there as guests of the Government we were offered the opportunity to go on safari in the south-west of the country.

'We arrived at the park and were given a tour in what I

would describe as a Jeep, a four-wheel-drive open-topped car. We had a park warden with us, who pointed out the animals – zebra, giraffe, even a pride of lions. In fact, while we were looking at the pride of lions to the left of the jeep there was another lion on the other side of the vehicle not ten feet from us, stalking what I believe it believed was a "truck full of rubbernecks".

'Anyway, suddenly from inside our jeep came the cry from Mr Maxwell: "We wish to see a rhinoceros!" Everyone, including the warden, scoured the horizon with their binoculars for a rhinoceros. Eventually the warden spotted one and we took off in its direction. The driver stopped the car a safe distance – about 40 yards or so – from the rhino. We were told to stay in the vehicle, and I must say I for one had no intention of doing anything else.

'Suddenly a door was flung open and Maxwell, accompanied by his trusty photographer, marched off in the direction of the rhinoceros.

'I was watching this with horror and consternation. First of all I am a law-abiding citizen and I didn't like to see the warden's rules being abused. Secondly there seemed to be a good deal of physical peril to the person I was responsible for, and thirdly his actions could be placing us all in some peril.

'As Maxwell approached the beast there began an exchange of eyeballing. The rhinoceros looked at Maxwell and carried on munching the meagre tuft of grass that had his attention. Maxwell advanced another five yards.

'I could see the rhinoceros studying Maxwell, and I could imagine it saying to itself: "Don't come any closer; that isn't what you do, it isn't playing the game. If you persist you will force me to uphold the formalities and charge. But it's a very hot day and I am busy, so please, bugger off."

'This didn't deter Maxwell, who advanced further. Again I could imagine the rhinoceros saying: "Now look here, this is unacceptable. If I allow you to get away with this it will set a bad precedent for all rhinoceroses. You are forcing me to make some show of remonstration, but surely we have all got better things to do, so kindly go away."

'Maxwell continued to advance and the rhinoceros fixed Maxwell with a steady gaze. From my position in the jeep I could hear the rhinoceros saying to itself: "Do we have to go through this? Perhaps if I move off a few yards he will get his photographs and go away."

'The rhinoceros duly obliged, but Maxwell followed.

'I thought: "This is now getting serious."

'Maxwell was about 30 yards from the jeep by now and the rhinoceros was about 30 yards beyond him. I calculated that by the time the rhinoceros had travelled 31 yards, Maxwell would have travelled one yard. So I shouted at him to get back into the truck, and so did the park warden. Maxwell paid no attention to us at all.

'Matters were quickly approaching a climax. As Maxwell approached the rhinoceros and the rhinoceros continued to keep an eye on the approaching publisher I could again imagine what was running through the mind of the rhinoceros: "This bugger will not back off. I have considered all the options and he leaves me no alternative. He is insulting me and my whole species and frankly I can't let him get away with it."

'At this point the rhinoceros turned to face Maxwell and they glowered at each other. I was thinking: "This man may be brave but he is entirely mad."

'Maxwell looked around to see that the photographer was in position. The rhinoceros was about to charge when suddenly I could hear it say to itself: "Bugger it!" The creature turned on its heel and galloped off. Maxwell returned to the car, the photographs of him staring out the rhinoceros duly taken. I'm sure if it came to it he would have stood his ground.'

*   *   *

Maxwell wasn't noted as a man who concerned himself about details; indeed he was said to have the attention span of a gnat. But he could focus his attention when he had to – and not only in business matters. One of his chauffeurs discovered this on his first day in the job. He was asked to go and collect Maxwell in the Rolls Royce. It was a sunny day and he'd wound down one of the windows, only to find that it wouldn't wind back. When he arrived at his destination to pick up Mr Maxwell he asked him if he knew what was wrong. His boss said that he did and promptly rolled up his shirt sleeves and fixed it.

John Featley recalls, 'He loved to be mothered, and if he was ill the whole world had to hear about it. If he caught a cold it seemed to hit him very hard. I suppose it was something to do with having only one lung and carrying all that weight.

'I remember one occasion at a bash held by the *Sunday Times*; it was Christmas 1989 and Mrs Maxwell had been having a go at me, telling me to look after her husband because he'd just got over a cold. It was a cold and wet night and I had to pick Mr Maxwell up from Stationers' Hall.

'When I arrived, I parked the Rolls immediately outside and took his hat and coat off the back seat before I went in. He was coming down the stairs and he'd got all of the people from the *Sunday Times* in tow.

'He spotted me and said: "John, what are you doing here?"

'"I've brought your hat and coat," I said. "Mrs Maxwell has told me to look after you because you've just got over a cold."

'He loved it.

'He turned to the crowd behind him and said: "They'll run your life if you let them."'

Maxwell's personal chef, Martin Cheeseman, travelled to Wyoming for Ian Maxwell's wedding. Next day Maxwell phoned Cheeseman and said: 'I'm going to take you somewhere you have never been before. We are going to picnic in Yellowstone National Park.'

'What he didn't tell me was that I was expected to provide

the picnic. So I made up a hamper of some of his favourite foods and we set off for the park. There was myself, Robert Maxwell, Mrs Betty Maxwell, his youngest daughter Ghislaine and a butler. We saw the main tourist attraction, the geyser Old Faithful, and then we sat down on the grass for our picnic. As we were all eating ice cream, Mrs Maxwell said: "Father," [she always referred to Maxwell like that], "Father," she said, "you are sitting by some stools." As she said it she pointed to some dark, round objects lying on the grass beside Mr Maxwell. He said: "They're not stools, that's buffalo shit!"

'We all laughed. It was a very enjoyable day out.'

* * *

During Maxwell's short association with the American whizkid Saul Steinberg (boss of Leasco), one of the characteristics which drew Steinberg to Maxwell was his sociability. He once remarked at a party in New York that Maxwell knew more people there than he did. Maxwell never stopped trying to make contacts. He never really had a social life: everything was geared towards business. One of his American butlers, James Tissot, remembers a lunch at the Helmsley Palace Hotel in New York which was hosted by Maxwell.

'The guest of honour was Armand Hammer, Chairman of the Occidental Oil Company. There were 14 people there altogether. I'm not sure about Maxwell's connections with the top people in Israel, but these guests could have been part of all that so I can't tell you their names. All I can say is that for a lot of Jewish people it was strange that they were having lobster [Jewish dietary laws forbid the eating of shell fish]. The staff figured conservatively that the combined wealth of the luncheon party had to be in excess of $20 billion.

'To Maxwell everything was measured in terms of money. If he had a party on the *Lady Ghislaine*, it was only successful if huge quantities of food and wine were consumed. I remember after one party (at which, incidentally, I heard him tell

Senator John Tower that he wouldn't be allowed to leave until he'd spoken to such and such a person) he boasted about how much caviar and Dom Perignon champagne had been consumed. He told me four and a half pounds of caviar had been eaten. In fact, I knew that only half of that had gone – the rest had been stolen by members of staff. So too had half of the very expensive champagne. So in his terms it wasn't a very successful party after all.'

*   *   *

Maxwell had a variety of chauffeurs. Jill Thompson, who was one of Maxwell's secretaries for a time, remembers the memorable day a new chauffeur was taking Maxwell from Headington Hill Hall to London. Maxwell was sitting in the back of the Rolls Royce. The car pulled up at some traffic lights and, without telling the driver, Maxwell stepped out – he'd seen a newspaper shop and decided to nip in and buy a paper. Unfortunately the chauffeur didn't realize his boss was no longer in the back of the car until he arrived at their destination in London.

*   *   *

When Maxwell was seized with an idea, nothing could deflect him. Once he was due to go to the Albert Hall for a concert to be attended by the Queen and at which he and Mrs Maxwell were due to be introduced to Her Majesty. As usual with Maxwell's travel arrangements he was running late. They were sitting in the back of the Rolls Royce and were about five minutes away from the Albert Hall when Maxwell suddenly asked the driver to pull over. He said: 'Get Mrs Maxwell a cab from here. I have to go somewhere urgently.'

Mrs Maxwell was astonished and said to her husband: 'What do you mean, you have to go somewhere urgently? We are going to meet the Queen!' Maxwell said he couldn't explain, but he just couldn't go and Mrs Maxwell would have to go on without him.

The driver said that they were so close to the Albert Hall that it would be easier to take Mrs Maxwell there than to find her a taxi. Maxwell agreed that this is what they should do. Mrs Maxwell was far from satisfied and pressed her husband for an explanation. None was forthcoming.

Then she returned to her previous argument and said: 'But we are due to meet the Queen. How do I explain why you're not there?'

'Tell her I'm a busy man!'

*   *   *

One day Maxwell was sitting at his desk in his penthouse apartment in Maxwell House. He looked up thoughtfully and asked one of his inner circle: 'Tell me, what does it feel like to be working for a man worth half a billion pounds?'

The employee responded by saying he'd never really thought about it, but was that how much Mr Maxwell was worth? Maxwell said that it was. Then he asked the employee if he would like to have wealth on such a scale. The man responded that it was always nice to have a little extra money but that he wouldn't know what to do with as much as that.

Maxwell looked wistful. 'Quite right – it doesn't buy you health or happiness.'

Not Maxwell Stories

Robert Maxwell enjoyed being famous. He enjoyed being talked about, as long as this created a favourable image. He was described by one union leader as 'a man who fills a room'. It's not surprising that fictional stories about him abound. I include a few of these not only because they are amusing but because they exhibit authentic flashes of Maxwell's character.

Maxwell was fond of a cigar. He often used to dip it into a brandy glass before lighting up and he wasn't always fussy whose brandy glass he used. In view of this, it comes as a surprise to learn that the great man was violently anti-smoking. He did not permit it in his presence and his employees were often encouraged to give it up or admonished for not doing so. He once offered a secretary £1,000 to stop. His son Ian – who was fond of a cigarette – would go to great lengths to clear the air in his office so that his father didn't realize he'd been smoking.

Now legend has it that one day Mr Maxwell was stalking the corridors of his empire when he came across a man in overalls having a sneaky drag. He went up to him and told him there was a no-smoking policy and that he should put out his cigarette.

The smoker said nothing. Maxwell then lectured him on the health risks. Still no response. Finally, Maxwell is said to have asked the man how much he earned. The smoker replied: '£200 a week.' Maxwell reached into his pocket and pulled out £800, saying: 'There's a month's wages. You're sacked.'

The man is said to have walked off feeling rather perplexed. He didn't like being told off and wondered whether or not to accept the money, but decided under the circumstances to do so – even though he didn't work for Maxwell!

This story has been told with different entrepreneurs taking the role of Maxwell and although many people I spoke to claimed it was true, none of them had witnessed it.

*   *   *

Maxwell was justifiably proud of his linguistic ability. He always maintained he learnt English in six weeks. He spoke French, German and Russian fluently and could understand a host of other languages. At one party in Headington Hill Hall, he is said to have been showing off by speaking to a variety of guests in their native tongues as they were leaving. The story concerns Lady Leach, the wife of Sir Ronald Leach – who before his knighthood was one of the Board of Trade Inspectors who dubbed Maxwell unfit to be a director of a publicly quoted company.

Anyway, Sir Ronald and Lady Leach were said to be at this party, which logic would of course suggest is hardly likely. Lady Leach, it's claimed, is fluent in Swahili. As she was leaving she addressed Maxwell in a language which he did not understand but which, rather than lose face, he pretended to.

Outside Headington Hill Hall Lady Leach was asked what she said to the publisher. She is supposed to have responded 'I said: "Thank you for the party. I hope we never see your like again."'

(I spoke to Sir Ronald Leach at his home in the Channel Islands, and he assured me his wife does not speak Swahili.)

*   *   *

Maxwell hired a man called John Egan as a Press Officer.

For some time afterwards legend has it he was very kind to the man, treating him almost with deference. Then one day after a meeting in which Egan was involved, Maxwell is supposed to have turned to an aide and said: 'Tell me, why have I hired the Chairman of Jaguar Cars?' (At the time a better-known John Egan was indeed Jaguar's chairman; now Sir John, he is currently Chairman of the British Airports Authority.)

This story is often told – though never by the aide to whom Maxwell addressed the question.

Epilogue

As I have mentioned already, I met Robert Maxwell only once. I wasn't with him long enough to form an opinion about what motivated him. But ever since the Seymour Hersh book I have been investigating Maxwell's affairs. I have travelled to Switzerland and Liechtenstein to try to unravel the complex web of his financial dealings, and in gathering anecdotes for this book I tried to understand the complex workings of Maxwell's mind. At the end of it I believe I do understand him a little better.

I think he changed little in the decades since he was a jewellery salesman in Czechoslovakia. He probably used unscrupulous methods then and he used them until he died. At first he was motivated mainly by money. But he quickly realized that what money brought him had a far more exotic taste – and in the end it was power that really interested him. What made Maxwell special was that he was prepared to work longer, to work harder, to be more unscrupulous than those around him. He was prepared to sacrifice everything and everybody in his pursuit of power. Nothing mattered to him but his belief that somehow he was special, and that somehow he must build a lasting monument to himself. It may perhaps have stemmed from deep-seated guilt because he survived the holocaust and most of his family perished.

I suppose that in the end he has achieved a sort of fame. Films are planned about him, books are written – there is even a Maxwell musical on the drawing-board. Until his sorry ending Maxwell's life really was a thing of dreams; the penniless peasant hunted by the Nazis who escapes, goes behind enemy lines disguised as a German, wins the Military Cross for bravery in the field, and then becomes an MP and a half-billionaire.

So what went wrong? When you have such self-belief and disregard everyone else's opinions, the possibility of disaster is never far away. It would be easy to say that his US deals invited disaster because he had borrowed the money and couldn't afford to pay it back. Interest rates kept on rising and the debt burden made the collapse of his empire inevitable. But in the past Maxwell had foreseen the fluctuations in the stock market. He had forecast crashes and advised others to bale out only weeks before disaster. So why didn't he see what was likely to happen in his own case?

Many people I spoke to believe that in the last year of his life there was a definite mental deterioration in Maxwell. There are examples of him forgetting that he'd sacked senior editorial staff and insisting that they were still working for him. Those close to him say he began to lose interest in business matters and was preoccupied more and more with parading himself as a world statesman. Could it really have been that he was on the verge of senility? And what about his death? Was it suicide, an accident, or murder? Many colleagues believe it was suicide. It is perhaps significant that it was the first trip aboard the yacht in which Maxwell had not taken a secretary or personal assistant.

But whatever happened, Maxwell left a hell of a mess behind him. He stole hundreds of millions of pounds of pensioners' money and he left many of them virtually destitute. He seems to have fulfilled his own prophecy, that none of his family would benefit from the wealth he created during his lifetime. But it is suggested that buried in Liechtenstein there could yet be many secret trusts, each dedicated to an individual member of his family, which may already have paid out large sums of money. What happened may never be fully discovered.

The mystery would have excited Maxwell. And it reminds me of another anecdote. Maxwell was known to have a weak bladder. When he landed by helicopter on the roof of the Mirror Building in Holborn he would often urinate over the edge and say, pointing at people 10 floors below:

'Look, I'm pissing on them and they don't even realize it.'

Some might think the words would make a fitting epitaph for Maxwell.